EMPIRE OF DISORDER

This work, published as part of a program of aid for publication, received support from the French Ministry of Foreign Affairs and the Cultural Service of the French Embassy in the United States.
Special Thanks to Giancarlo Ambrosino and Brian Dermot O'Keefe

Semiotext(e)
2571 W. Fifth Street
Los Angeles, CA 90057
www.semiotexte.org

Semiotext(e)
501 Philosophy Hall
Columbia University
New York, NY 10027

Distributed by The MIT Press, Cambridge, Mass. and London, England
Design: Hedi El Kholti

ISBN: 978-1-58435-016-3

EMPIRE OF DISORDER

ALAIN JOXE

Translated by Ames Hodges
Edited by Sylvère Lotringer

SEMIOTEXT(E) ACTIVE AGENTS SERIES

CONTENTS

FOREWORD

Special circumstances, no doubt, have affected the state of the world since September 2001: in New York City, the attack on the Twin Towers symbolizing the economic and financial power of the Empire, and in Washington the attack on the Pentagon, which represents its military power. With the invention of a terrorism at once suicidal and genocidal by a renegade CIA network, the Bin Laden sect, which turned three airplanes into cruise missiles, everything seems to have changed.

But this is not a circumstantial book. It seemed important, even before September 11, to assess for what they were the years that followed the Gulf War. The circumstances surrounding the investiture of President Bush, the oil president; the break-down of the Israeli-Palestinian peace process with the new Intifada; the projection of NATO into Central Asia through the unprecedented Russia-NATO Act; the exaction carried out by the Taliban regime; all of these events foretold trouble in the East-West / North-South crossroads of the Greater Middle East.

This essay is a strategic and political review of the twelve years following the Gulf War. I have included certain reflections that arose during the Balkan disasters and that are necessary to ground more targeted analyses that must also be done of each of the atrocious little wars and broken-down peace that keep on emerging in the 21st century in all the zones of the "South."

Strategic criticism must turn the violent events of the bloodiest wars into an occasion for clarification rather than ignorance and anguish. Criticism is always possible and necessary since the rationality of war is *imperfect*, to the extent that it is not solely guided by reason. It almost always involves the passions of soldiers or the imagination of assassins. If political violence were passionless, like the cold SS administration of the concentration camps, it would be perfect violence, pure destruction adapted to its inhuman results and in no way connected to its human causes. It would require no explanations and be a source of permanent fear. But passions are inevitable as long as *victory does not take sides*. And fighting continues for humanity throughout the globe between soldiers for whom the superiority of one side over the other can only be proven by a fight to the death. Violence is always fiery, as long as it remains a combat opposing adversaries who identify themselves by their hatred of the other and who give their life out of love for those like themselves. Violence is always linked to human passion, even in the instant of ultra-rapid death.

This traditional form of violence and its accompanying hatred, love, madness and repentance have not disappeared. On the contrary, it is thriving in Africa, Asia, Latin America, in the Balkans and the Caucases. The geographic prevalence of armed violence in the *Souths* should not lead us to think that these are new examples of "cultural savagery": they are the result of a strategy by the dominant countries to spatialize violence and push the most virulent causes of violence into the South. Something they did not know how to do during the two World Wars.

Philosophers do not always have the nerve to face these real problems in real time. A number of them think they can rid themselves of the problem by describing it as a return of the "archaic," and imagining that history or the past are the direct causes of today's conflicts. Yet even philosophers are less inclined to participate in this sort of escape from reality than our modern, logical, civilized politicians, our most Cartesian leaders. This fact became obvious during the war in Bosnia: in good faith, no doubt, politicians invented from scratch an entire segment of history, a traditional, secular struggle between Serbs and Croats that had never existed.

"Traditional" violence is quickly categorized as pathological. And in a way it is true: the horrors of war can be described as an accumulation of acts of individual madness. Or as the diseased regression—because deficient and irrational—of underdeveloped societies towards ancient behavior. But this culturalist judgement merely censures or obliterates the traditional violence and common barbarity that were prevalent in Europe at least until the end of the 19th century, if not the 20th with Nazism and colonial wars.

Calling barbaric violence cultural or pathological is contrary to the political definition of the causes of political violence. In fact, it is necessary to trace the distinctly modern political and sociological causes of wars today, for it is only in that way that the possibility of assigning *responsibilities* and establishing methods of political *prevention* can be considered. Given the "barbarity" of current wars, if we admit that their causes are current, then we must also realize that the worst is always possible. Under certain conditions, political violence could develop with hellish rationality and passionless organization; those responsible for it would accept to commit *cruelty without hatred* and without fear. Memories of the Nazi period should allow us to picture this evolution as possible anywhere in the world, just as it was possible in Europe under the reign of Hitler. Global barbarity would certainly take the above form under the following circumstances:

First condition: If the *reciprocal* death threats between conflicting cultural identities disappeared and were replaced by an overwhelming, unilateral, completely asymmetrical menace, and if subordinate strategic identities were all combined, in a general "oppressive globality," or suffered in perpetual submission. The legitimacy of this system would come from the recognition, without combat, of the absolute superiority of a single dominant power and the acceptance at every level of sub-contracts to carry out massacres.

Some of the harshest military dictatorships in Latin America and Asia—in Argentina, Uruguay, Chile, South Korea, Indonesia— already furnish long-standing examples of sub-contracted massacres centrally organized by the United States during the Cold War. But each of these armies believed at the time that they were loyal cogs in the grand strategic vision of "the struggle against Communism." In Latin America, it has been confirmed that various systems of selective and somewhat tentative *socio-political genocides* were organized directly by order and with the technical assistance of the United States secret services, in order to liquidate, based on probability studies, a certain type of leftist figure according to a unified doctrine of National Security (though this doctrine was still aimed at maintaining the framework of the Nation-State). This occurred in both Argentina and Chili. These examples give us an idea of what the vast centralized pyramid of asymmetrical massacre management might look like, the cold violence of globalist repression in the imperial system that has succeeded the bipolar world.

Certain cases in the most rigid Communist dictatorships, in moments of transition, also evoke the cold violence of Nazism. For example, in China during the Cultural Revolution (as it was and not as it should have been), and in the Pol Pot regime in Cambodia or the decline of the North Korean regime.

Second condition: Passionless barbarity could become global if violence were completely entrusted to machines instead of people, who would as a result become "servants" rather than "fighters," calm and clean in white collars behind their computers. The rationality of techno-strategy would then reach its zenith, without even obeying a global political project. Selective massacre would become the abstract bureaucratic act meant to maintain a police state with no *political* aim (*Zweck*), in other words without the goal of compelling defeated parties to agree at the negotiation table, or surrender without conditions, to a project of a future political order that would impose *an acceptable life on the losers*.

At an intermediary level, one finds the colonial massacres and tortures carried out by French, British and Portuguese decolonizers, the cruel exploits and Russian behaviors in the Chechen War, the militias and "tchetnik" nationalist troops of Mladic and Karadzic or Milosevic and Seselj and the "oustachis" of Mate Boban, as well as the partial post-colonial genocides of crumbling African regimes, all of which were organized *coldly* but executed *ardently* by elite troops closer in stature and mentality to the SA than the SS.

In each of the above cases, the source of military rationality, its *political* source, would disappear, replaced by something else, by a technique for constant management of a calculated massacre as an act aimed at *directly regulating*, not politics—since such an *art* would obviously be the negation of any political community, or else a political definition of the corporation—but *demographics and the economy*.

This scenario will not occur soon, even though we can begin to see its line of flight towards the horizon of global violence traced in the current automation of weaponry and in connection with the globalization of financial capital and the "sovereignty of corporations" leading to *involuntary* social catastrophes. Or, put in another way: this concomitance between two global automations must be fought politically.

A strategic approach can help define the struggle—against the *simultaneousness* of these two *automations*—since one would be hard pressed to find any living and breathing proponents of this grisly future. Yet throughout the world, circulating the hallways, one can find the reports, the fictions, the fragments of partial speech that resemble the virus or genes or mitochondria of a Nazi code being formed in the primal soup of global neo-liberalism.

But by recognizing that the world has explicitly become a "chaos" under the pressure of neo-liberalism, we become aware that other possible worlds might be better, and we can call the future of the American Empire into question, from the critical point of view of the defense of Republics against Empires.

We must convince ourselves that the legitimate form of resistance against the Empire has to remain the social Republic and that throughout Europe, the tools are there to carry out this program, as long as they are used to form a strategy for the future and not a regression back to the imperial homelands of the 19th century. Very important contradictions, which are becoming patent, appear between the values, objectives and means of the globalist Empire and those of the European Republics.

Even without explicit proclamations, European citizens are pursuing a different project than the neo-liberal American Empire. In order to state these differences clearly, I will start by offering a genealogy of the model of the social Republic. To ask the right questions, we have to return to the strategic foundations of the Republic and the Empire as they took shape in the West, starting with Machiavelli, Hobbes and Clausewitz—though they were preceded by Marsilius of Padua and Dante.

We will see how to evaluate what chances the Republic—born in England in 1649 and consolidated in 1688 then reincarnated in the United States in 1774-77 and in France in 1789-93—still has currency as a model capable of resisting the global Empire, not like an exclusive claim [*Jacobin*], but as a general model of democratic sovereignty. The essence of the state and also of the Empire, in other words the state when it seeks to become a universal monarchy, until today has been the protection against war, a protection that the Sovereign owes citizens and allies, especially if the Sovereign is the People. I will discuss this point further in the chapters that give Hobbes' reflections on protection and Clausewitz's considerations on the "continuation" of politics through war an active conceptual role in the current state of affairs.

The United States, however, as an imperial power, today refuses to assume the protective role for its friendly or dominated auxiliaries. It does not seek to *conquer* the world and take responsibility for protecting the subjugated societies. Yet it is nonetheless at the head of an empire, though this empire is merely a system for *regulating disorder* by means of financial norms and military expeditions and has no intention to occupy conquered territories. It operates on a case-by-case scenario, organizing repression of the symptoms of despair, applying almost the same norms both internally and externally.

The question is often asked whether the power of the United States is primarily economic or primarily military and in what "proportions" or in what mode. In short, what is the definition of the global political domination it has established under the name of "globalization" that leads to increased disparities between rich and poor, to the rise of an international, rootless "noble caste" and to an escalating number of endless wars?

The United States had in fact been preparing itself theoretically ever since the Gulf War, or at least for the past five years, for something new that they had foreseen in principle. Certain think tanks and groups of experts, closer to the Army and the Marines, understood that the absolute superiority gained by their mastery of the practical effects of the electronic revolution, both in the military, aero-satellite sphere and the economic and financial sphere, would lead, with "globalization," to qualitatively intolerable asymmetrical effects. They realized that the counterattack by the nations, peoples and classes sacrificed would take unexpected forms and sometimes the form of terrorism, the weapon of the weak. This counterattack would most likely require heightened inventiveness, and the United States was supposed to head them off in order to protect itself. This was the origin of the general concept of an "asymmetrical war."

Theoretical strategy[1] is used here to confront the concept of globalism because we will have to defend ourselves against the

Empire of Disorder, and this discipline can be applied like an anthropology and a logic of reciprocal action under the threat of death. It assumes that relations of force are based in part on *imaginary* representations during the period of deterrence and prevention, but also during the period of operations. Imaginary means imagined, not unrealistic.

In times like today the strategic approach must be renewed: since the dawn of time, it ordinarily seeks to evaluate rationally the representations and actions of states in violent interaction, but with a unique system of leadership imposing its norms on a world considered to be a semi-unpredictable chaos, the problems of *hierarchization* or *victory* it elicits are formally different than those that arise from free competition between states regulated by agreements and international common law.

This transnational imperial leadership requires the maintenance of what state traditions keep calling disorder while pushing it to the outskirts of the Empire. However, the limits of the imperial system today are no longer geographical and disorder can be found everywhere.

It clearly appears that the American strategy of avoiding the responsibility of protecting socio-economically societies of geographical nation-states and their operational strategy of *repressing* the symptoms of despair—rather than attacking its causes—leads us straight into an impasse or to the rise of a global anti-democratic regime. The first steps were taken with the globalist strategies initiated under Clinton and have been confirmed under Bush Jr. The Empire, on the economic offensive under Clinton, is now taking the completely new form of a military and expeditionary offensive.

Offering this prospect leads to the certain failure, though not necessarily close, of the attempts to establish global deregulation and to redefine a "monopolar" American Empire as an Empire of Disorder. I defend the idea that Europe, as a pluralist power and a crossroads of continents, probably represents the primary line of resistance to this empire for structural, and not only ideological reasons, but also for political and security reasons as well.

Until now, the hope for peace has been at the root of the imagination of war. In fact, "peace is normally the goal of war. On the contrary, war is not the goal of peace," as Saint Augustine once told us. If the interior peace of a state is some times restored by the *invention* of an external threat of war, this exportation of violence owes more to a hellish peace than a divine one. If it is true that we have entered the era when globalization will erase the frontiers between internal and external wars, we can also anticipate that it will either eliminate peace or preferably that it will erase the boundary between internal peace and external peace, so that peace can become the global objective for eliminating war.

Current wars now appear to be managed like wars of repression by "liberal states" against "terrorism," but this is a temporary appearance, due mostly to the American media effort that requires its allies to demonstrate their solidarity in strange or even absurd terms corresponding to the American view of the outside world, an extreme neo-Darwinist, behaviorist and autistic view of their "tribal wisdom" that was understandable for a family of pioneers penetrating the plains of the Far West, but highly defective for those who would seek universal royalty.

Because terrorism is not an adversary, only a form of political violence, its suppression is not a Clausewitzian political goal that could end in a victory and a peace, especially since counter-terrorist actions are always implicated in a state or imperial terrorism and violations of human rights, measures that are the source of the most extreme forms of resistance and of terrorism itself. Without attacking the causes, we reinforce the cycle.

Republics, forms of sovereignty that we return to here to find a contemporary meaning in their origins, normally should come together on a global level to stop this hopeless cycle and resist this imperial chaos.

ALAIN JOXE / SYLVÈRE LOTRINGER, A DIALOGUE

1. Civil Wars Everywhere

Frozen Peace □ Chaos and Complexity □ Decomposition of
Communism □ Re-making of the State □ Regions, not Religions
□ Kosovo □ Free Market Economy □ Shaping the World □
"Knowing Everything" □ The "Detaillist" Era □ "Panopolitics"
□ Ruling the World □ Colombia and Algeria □ "United Europe"
□ Technological Military Domination □ Neo-Liberalism and
Fascism □ Absolute Domination □ Conquest and Defeat □
American Incompetence □ Military Keynesianism □
"Revolution in Military Affairs" □ "Good Governance" □
Corporate Culture □ Ethnic Wars Are Class Wars

You're talking about frozen peace, but wouldn't it be more appropriate to say that war has been frozen?

Yes, you could say that, except when the war *escalates* during the peace process, as is the case, for example, in Colombia. There is a peace process in place and at the same time massacres are increasingly frequent, the adversaries are strengthening their arsenals. You have a peace process that is also a process of expanding war.

Do the massacres concern soldiers or, as in the case of Yugoslavia and especially in Kosovo, mostly the civilian population with limited military casualties?

With civil wars, it is hard to distinguish between the two. Moreover, one of the reasons for these massacres is that the wars are always civil wars in any case. The fiction of religious wars does not quite work… For stupid or unfortunate reasons, even for barbaric ones, in all inter-ethnic wars there is always an aspect of civil war. And when there is a traditional civil war, in other words a war between classes, or in any case between distinct socio-political alliances, the question of activism is frequently raised, sometimes religious activism.

It seems that there has been an increase in civil wars, inter-ethnic wars, religious wars since the end of the Cold War. Is that true, or have they become more visible because the two blocs no longer exist?

It is more visible because the two blocs are no longer there and because the colonial empires have disappeared as well.

The fragmentation of the Soviet bloc allowed the formation or expression of all kinds of disputes and conflicts that were mostly contained before…

It is true that the dissolution of empires produces little wars, Balkanizations, Lebanonizations, things of that nature. We can ask ourselves, however, if there really are more of them, or if there has only been a change in perception. The disturbances and their suppression used to take place inside the empires. They did not produce what we call wars; they were called rebellion and repression. And then, liberation.

They may also be given far more prominence, at least temporarily, through real-time information. In the "global-city" everything has become more visible.

Yes, it is clear that there was no television coverage of the war in Chechnya and the repression of the Chechens by Stalin. Television, the end of the colonial empires and the end of bipolar confrontation all combine to cause local phenomena to proliferate. In the past, local phenomena were filed under the East-West conflict. The war in Angola or in Mozambique was like a part of the Cold War; no one was going to cover it constantly.

The war was understood before being analyzed...

Yes, you could always say it's the East's fault or it's the West's fault. Whereas everything now becomes a study of complexity. It is tiring for politicians, but interesting for journalists because everything turns out to be something special. You have to send someone with a minimum understanding of the situation. It is more complicated, but nothing is more complicated than nothing.

You have to start with chaos then.

No, you have to start with complexity. Chaos is a global idea, but locally situations are generally less chaotic than they appear to the world in general. If you did a thorough and detailed analysis of the situation in Colombia, you would say the war there is extremely cruel but not incomprehensible. Analyzing the situation of the Palestinians would produce the same results. Russia is naturally more complex and appears more chaotic because of its greater size.

In Russia, there is a territorial conflict at the same time as an ethnic or religious conflict.

But everywhere in Russia the actors express themselves using clear language and through debates in the press, even under very barbaric circumstances. The most obscure places are perhaps Bosnia because we do not understand the nature of the real motivations. The Serbs' will to "ethnic cleansing" seemed to appear out of nowhere in a country where, on the contrary, communities used to be happily mixed together. That is a mystery… It can only be solved by a detailed understanding of the birth of Yugoslavia in the war of liberation.

There is also the death of Tito. The end of the amalgam he managed to maintain under the banner of an alternative Communism let all kinds of elements emerge that are hard to understand, of an ethnic order, etc. What is important is the decomposition of Communist power. That is the new element.

That is new. Communist power once was composed and now it has decomposed. Whether this decomposition is ethnic in origin or religious or something else, no one can say since it has always been like that in the Balkans independently of Communism. It is not because there are religious structures that seem to work like political identities that the religious structures are an explanation. In fact, the primary explanation follows from the decomposition of the Communist systems that were established after the war. Including those that, like Titoism, came from an autonomous movement of resistance fighters—they owed nothing to the Russians, in any case, and little to the British—in the struggle against the Nazis, that was reproduced after Tito took power. We might have had certain keys for understanding the Soviet invasion of Czechoslovakia and the liberation of Czechoslovakia from Soviet influence, but for Yugoslavia, we have no keys to understand this decomposition and even the Yugoslavians have been left dumbfounded.

It can nonetheless be understood in terms of territorial ambition, national identity, power struggles…

It can be explained in terms of a crisis of the state. A sort of will to power was formed in certain sectors of the Yugoslavian *nomen-clatura*, who were the ones to hold power from the beginning. Then things went bad and in some countries it turned into a sort of aggressive and extremely nationalist fascism, which is contrary to Titoism. They kept the organizational structures and increased the police forces, it became a fascist dictatorship. But since it was accompanied by a transition to democracy due to the breakdown of the single party system, we are left puzzled because then we have to invent the concept of the democratically elected fascist dictatorship… Even Hitler cannot help us understanding it since the elections he won involved a single party. So you invent things, and then you think: why use the word fascist at all? Simply because there is no other word, because there are armed groups that are not part of the army and that have the right to kill people on the street. I call that fascism, which is by the way the definition of *fascio*: armed groups. They are paramilitaries, they have special uniforms, they are militias. And you have the same thing happening everywhere else, in Colombia, in Algeria…

The black squadrons…

… who actually do perform barbaric acts and spread terror…

... and who often serve a state.

Yes, yes. But what is not said is that it is not in the service of a state, but of a *state in search of itself.* First there is the decomposition of the previous state—we know very well that we cannot speak of a revolution in the factual sense. There is the destruction of the Titoist state: what happens then? A revolution, not merely that ensuing states are republics. No, a state is something you destroy, something you rebuild. It has not been completely rebuilt, moreover, because you still had militias in Yugoslavia, at least in the states that had inherited from it. There was Milosevic, there was the army, but there were militias, which is proof that the state had not quite been rebuilt yet because there was no absolute monopoly on legitimate violence. And the militias were barbaric, more SA than SS. What Hitler did during "The Night of the Long Knives" was to liquidate the SA as an uncontrolled militia; and the SS, they were the state.

He had to provide guarantees to the German military...

The military had to have guarantees, right, because the military still remained a force. And the Serbian army... You can make all the comparisons you like, but if we hold that the decomposition takes us back to clan rivalry, etc., we miss the fact that a very precise political maneuver took place. First between the Serbs and Croats to create a nationalist war, then the Serbs and Croats made an agreement, and then finally Bosnia was attacked. But there were maneuvers to destroy every multi-ethnic society of cities like Vukovar—the Serbo-Croatian town that was liquidated, along with Mostar, with its Croats and Muslims. The militias that wreaked terror had to be launched from villages where ethnic memories were still present, since in the cities the memories had no meaning, and *then* the terror spread to the city. I had a student who got her degree by doing remarkable work on that subject. She went there and did surveys on location, asking people how the killing started. These elements show that it was a crisis of the Communist State and a reappropriation by certain elites that you could call Thermidorian since they took away and privatized everything to their own advantage, thus becoming ultra-nationalist elites. All the members were former Communists, which means that Communism already was in crisis since Communism is not nationalism, or in any case shouldn't be. Their allies were plain bandits like Arkan, leader of a football gang.

Nationalism breaks things apart, but it pulls things together too. Tito used Yugoslavian nationalism for his own purpose...

Tito constantly struggled against nationalism to the extent that it threatened to explode Titoist Yugoslavia.

But there was Yugoslavian nationalism as well in opposition to Russia.

Yes, that's right. There was a first hint of Yugoslavian nationalism, let's say of a national identity. And it was blown apart. Naturally enough, neither the Americans nor the Europeans wanted that to happen. At first even the United States was against the idea. Then they went along with it, but it was not part of the program.

How do you think the Americans reacted then? How did they adapt to the situation? After all, they ended up stepping in ...

They took their time to intervene. Actually this is a subject that could benefit from further study, but at first they said, and rightly so, that they had no particular interest in the matter. Meaning there was no oil. "The lignite mines in Kosovo do not normally interest us, but it can be explosive." So they did not want to intervene because their doctrine was starting to take shape, their doctrine of no ground intervention as characteristic of American intervention. "We won't send ground forces unless there is a pre-established peace agreement allowing intervention." They did not want to intervene for the Europeans since it was *their* area. At first the Europeans did not want to intervene either. They had not yet organized themselves into a centralized power; the European Union did not exist in 1992, so there has been some progress since that time. This happened at the start of the process; the EEC was there, but not the European Union.

In a way, the Yugoslavian crisis accelerated the process of European unification.

There have been changes in European identity that may be the consequence of the need to confront the Yugoslavian problem. At present, European identity is more established and takes defense into account, and that comes mainly from Kosovo. Greater political and diplomatic identity became somewhat apparent during the Bosnian affair, but it was still weak.

There were nonetheless conflicting interests between the United States and, for example, France, or at least certain European countries.

Yes, but there was no debate. The true problems were never formulated, only false ones. For example, it was said that France was pro-Serb. For President François Mitterrand, that was true, but it was not quite true of France as a nation, or in terms of reasoning about the state. France could not be pro-Serb since it was a state that was murdering women and children. Pro-Serb meant being pro-Chetnik, but we could not be pro-Chetnik like Milosevic. The grand orchestra of Yugoslavia was convened, the baton was held by Milosevic. To stop the war, we negotiated with Milosevic so that he would get rid of Karadzic, but the problems entailed by this position did not become completely clear until Kosovo. Because then Milosevic was alone. Before, in the Bosnian war Milosevic could say, "I am intervening on the behalf of the Serbs, but I am not the one who provoked the secession, it is the Croats." The Americans didn't handle the situation right; the Europeans didn't handle it right either. We were not ready to face up to something that complex because we did not have an analysis of what the decomposition of a Communist system accompanied by the rebuilding of national criteria might be like. You cannot eliminate Communism and eliminate every nation-state at the same time. It's too much to ask of a nation. No one asked Poland to eliminate Poland. For federations like Russia or Yugoslavia, breaking down the Communist State has been more destructive.

All the more so that everyone, from the Russians to the Germans, has always done exactly that to Poland.

In the case of Yugoslavia, destroying Communism *and* nation had to be done at once, and it was impossible. Types of nationalism therefore redeveloped that were grotesque from the point of view of their real capacity for autonomy, since all the states depend on the European economy, just as European states depend on each other. Serbia and little bits of Croatia could only find their autonomy by depending on Mafia funds. So they did not exactly have the brightest future in store for them.

Which is also the case in Albania.

It's also true of Albania.

Except that Albania has a state.

True, but a state in crisis. It was pushed into a modernization that turned everything into a series of absolutely grotesque Mafia groups, and it almost sank completely. It is true that Albania is also a problem, but one that was not dealt with in the same way as Yugoslavia, it is less serious…

It had some noticeable effect on the Kosovo affair, as was discovered somewhat late when Albanians started taking repressive measures against Serbs in Kosovo.

That is not so clear. There is a big difference between the Albanians in Albania and the Albanians in Kosovo. The ones in Kosovo underwent ten years of military occupation and had to develop a parallel economy in order to survive. The parallel economy was supported by the diasporas, including the Mafias. People survive as best they can. What is important is primarily that they succeeded in ending clan warfare and therefore creating a national consensus and ending the reign of the vendetta. That was the beginning of the creation of the city-state in Europe along with the foundation of the tribunal, bringing an end to the vendettas between noble families symbolized by the Eumenides, and getting rid of Antigone and her histories…

That's right. It was the foundation of Athens.

Correct, it's Athens at the beginning. They had done that. So, in principle, the Kosovars had held elections—clandestinely—and normally they should have moved to the stage of democracy. They clearly were much better prepared for democracy, which they had practiced as an act of popular resistance against a foreign oligarchy. Better prepared, naturally, than the Albanians of Albania.

And than Serbians of Serbia.

And than Serbia, it goes without saying.

What they wanted in fact was independence.

Yes, that's right. It is really the place that deserves democratic independence. It was the same maybe for Bosnia, or for what was left of it. They had moved beyond clan divisions and wanted democracy.

This situation resembles the one Hobbes was in that you describe in this book: coming out of disorder in search of a formal state.

Yes, but then Europeans and Americans were forced to think about something: finally the two locations that suffered the most—and were actually mostly inhabited by Muslims—were people who had prepared themselves rather well for the passage to democracy. Whereas on the other side you had a bunch of Christians whose minds were set on killing their neighbors, despite the contradiction with the principal message of Christ. Therefore, these were not wars of religion, let's not anyone bother us with that. In any case, if it was a religious war, it did not fit the idea we have of the Christian and Muslim religions. I'm not talking about Islamism...

These religions have been used for various nationalist goals.

This war was designed with the intention of recreating violent segments of identity to replace the disappearance of the single-party Communist State. To do so, an ethnico-fascist single party system was needed. And alright, Tudjman tried, but he did not succeed since Croatia is mixed up in nearby Western affairs. Milosevic did not succeed in creating a single party but he did create an extreme nationalist party and a single police force. Those regions, not religions, work that way.

In each case, the ones who got it most were Muslims on the path to democracy.

They were on track to democracy perhaps because they were forced to think of themselves as oppressed minorities, or in Bosnia as a relative majority. But the same was true of the Protestants and Jews in France who made the Republic secular. The connection is not really to religion but rather to the particular situation that a religion can represent in the case of an identity that was not completely scattered.

To a certain extent, defending Kosovo meant defending a democracy that was about to take shape. And that is what we helped crush.

Of course, it is hard to talk about it now because the presence of a headless international mandate, armies with no head or tail occupying the country and NGOs (Non-Governmental Organizations) who get paid with international salaries, creates a certain international oligarchy, one that is not favorable to the birth of democracy. It's a protectorate. And moreover, there is

no centralized interpretative perspective like that of Lyautey or
any other figure, including that of the Third Republic in
Lebanon, that would say: "Here, we are going to make ourselves
a democracy"—out of what? But it has to be done. In Lebanon,
they did it by tinkering with the religious communities. There,
since they all speak the same language and share the same religion,
the representatives of the Third Republic would have had to recreate a normal electoral-type of democracy, with parties: a Rugova
party. Rugova is a little soft and an U.C.K. party a little Mafioso,
but that exists in our cities as well, groups made of people who are
a little Mafiosi and others who are somewhat soft democratic
thinkers. And then there would have been a few extremists, somewhat extreme-left, very solid—that's what a democracy is. And
there would have been conditions from the World Bank to eliminate the Mafia, linking the future of the country to this elimination.
Well, U.C.K. would have become a party with a military past, not
a very long one either, and a vision of the Albanian nation as a
divided nation. He would be required to have a specific policy for
Albanians from Albania, and there you have it. When they go to
Holland, the Flemish speak Dutch…

But now instead of all that we are having a frozen peace situation.

Yes.

Now, since we are at it, what do mean exactly by that?

It is a peace in the sense that it issues from an international
agreement. But in fact this is not a peace, it is a cease-fire. The
political conditions that have to be imposed on the conquered
party don't exist because no one has been conquered. No one

wanted to create a loser, so they created someone who was defeated, but not conquered. The same thing happened with Iraq. Saddam Hussein was beaten, but not conquered. As a result, the conditions of a negotiation bringing the war to an end had no reason to exist. So there were no peace negotiations.

It was a "non-war."

It's a "non-peace." Dayton is a so-called peace agreement, but it is not a peace agreement, it's the same. It does not matter what you call it. Now I think that even in the United States, they are starting to realize it. There is a critique of Dayton that is shared by Europeans, at least rhetorically, and Americans, and this is the point of departure for the initiative called the Stability Pact for South-East Europe—which is not a pact, by the way.

And it is recent.

Yes. It dates precisely from the day before Milosevic accepted to consider himself defeated. And thus negotiated the retreat of his troops. That was in June 1999. Which means it was worked out ahead of time. There already was prior reflection in Europe and maybe in the United States, or the United States came around to European thinking—they pretended like it was the other way around, but we know it isn't true. Still there was a sort of agreement that something else needed to be done besides the peace treaties that simply drew the lines of a cease-fire, and that a larger area must be taken into account. Naturally, that met the glorious American vision of an "enlargement" of the mercantile system and therefore vast spaces were needed to make solid large marches that were quantity-intensive. Only that is harder to do when there are wars and when there are cease-fire lines. And the Europeans think that this space needs to be rebuilt, not too quickly, by recreating contacts between neighbors, good neighbors and real relationships of reconstruction in which the state is not eliminated. The Americans are oriented less towards states, naturally, and more inclined to promote "grand functions" between states. And the money will come from the Europeans…

For Kosovo?

For the entire Balkan area, including Serbia once it became democratic. But that was already the case for Montenegro, even though it was a part of Serbia, because it was already being separated…

Sounds like the theory of the stages leading to Communism…

That's right, there are stages, but I don't know if they are as well regulated as the stages provided for by Marxism…

Not that they worked so well really…

The idea of stages remains, but I don't think that it is conceived of in the same way in Europe and in the United States, and this could lead to an important debate.

In Europe, it all goes through the state, while the United States does not need the state. They only need the fluxes to flow… as long as they are the first to profit from them.

There are people in the United States who think otherwise. You have debates in the United States that do not deal with this question theoretically, but in practice they are concerned with knowing whether they want to destroy states or not, at least not every time. Even if you are not for the state, when you say that a minimum state is necessary, you mean that the state should not get involved in the economy.

At least not outwardly. Or not all the time.

But a state that does not get involved in the economy does not exist. If you think that the American state is not involved in the economy, you are kidding yourself. But even that is not very clear.

Given the current state of things, everything that is connected with free trade, with economic neo-liberalism, goes America's way.

The state officially intervenes in favor of free trade, but to them it seems like a non-intervention. If you add a little historical depth and political culture here, from the European perspective, you will find it to be a pretty limited way of seeing things. It is obvious, and all the American leaders say so, that this intervention is intended to "shape" [*mettre en forme*] social and political forms. *Shaping* is the catchword of the moment: "to shape the world," "to shape Europe"... And if this is not politics, what is it? Politics does not disappear; it is merely relegated to "shaping" the political world so that it is favorable to direct action by corporations. This version of things is certainly not prohibited, but you cannot say that it is a non-political policy. It is politics. It is social politics, economic politics, but also military politics. And there is the shaping carried out by a military presence. "Making the state," at the same time, means making the army, the politics and the conditions of the economy. In the encounter between a European project for the Balkans and an American project for the Balkans, normally, there should have been a nice debate that would have been completely real...

On "shaping"...

...on shaping—what do we mean by "shaping"? If there is no agreement on what we mean by shaping, there will be confusions, even open conflicts, and in any case, frozen peace in the projection zones.

Exactly. The United States yet has to find their shape. At the moment it might happen through the war in Iraq, Kosovo, or independently of real conflicts in the field. It might not even be shaping a military conception of political strategy.

Yes, but we have to suspend our judgment about that topic a bit. If you say that the military is very important, you have to say that it is absolutely fundamental because it represents the threat of death. And the threat of death is essential for creating power. But the problem is that this threat of death is not aimed at conquering. The Americans refuse to take a territory by military means and install their troops to resolve political problems.

What they want is the world.

They want the world, but they don't want to invade the world. Their military action is therefore intended to manage the world by using this threat. But to do what? When the economy is the objective, you could say that the objective is not exactly to create the reign of a pure free market in the world, because what reign would be a market open under a threat and regulated by that threat. Of course, if you say that to Americans, they won't recognize their generous, democratic country; but strategically, that is what comes down the pipeline. This worries even the American military. Even in reference to Kosovo, they were saying: "We are being sent to do a mission, we do not know why. What is this 'military revolution?'" And they will never be able to specify why it is the way I said. Obviously a democracy like the United States could never say: "This is our strategy." However, if the overt strategy is to bring dictatorships to an end and to establish democracy throughout the world—because that is what is being said—then they should say: "Listen, we're sending our armies, but they are there to re-establish democracy against regimes like the Milosevic regime, who is a fascist, etc...."

But you cannot say that this strategy interested them very much when there were dictatorships all over Latin America.

Well, it is hard to comprehend why they have taken such a belated interest in it. In fact, the mystery is still greater now that we can see their material interests. The lignite in Kosovo still does not interest the American system, what interests them is American interests as they have developed over the past ten years. In other words, their interest in showing their military leadership and in saying that it is good for them means that military leadership is essential for the economy. But this interest is global; the local relationship is not always explicit. It could not really be seen in Kosovo since its presence was not directly predatory.

Couldn't we talk in terms of the attempt to erect a new system of deterrence—since you are a specialist in deterrence—something that wouldn't be on par with an atomic threat, but would be the threat of this unbeatable technological and computerized force?

Yes, it is a sort of threat of coercion through a form of ubiquitous, "detailist" presence. Foucault and Bentham's panopticon could be relevant here, obviously, because you have both the capability of reconnaissance and of targeting. And in this case, there is a sort of paranoia, of complete domination of every *scale* of the planet, the macro, meso, micro levels, etc. Local demonstrations of reconnaissance and targeting capabilities have a global strategic value.

Some time ago Kissinger bluntly stated in the Le Nouvel Observateur: *"We have chosen to know everything, be aware of everything." So they have ten thousand people in Washington who analyze everyday all the images, all the messages for the Pentagon. Or at least that is the picture they paint for us.*

Yes and no. If I wasn't convinced that Kissinger were a very intelligent man, I would say that he was crazy. So if he says that, he cannot be serious. I think he is kidding.

It is a form of deterrence... People have to think that they can control everything, that is part of deterrence, isn't it?

I'm not so sure. Deterrence cannot rely on absolute security alone, it must rely on the capability of punishing the things you were not able to control. So if you think you can control everything, you will have to punish absolutely minuscule things all the time and that's really tiring—you not only need observers, satellite decoders but also a lot of cops...

You always need enemies...

Just a second. In principle the enemies will be ironed out of the smooth world of harmonic trade. But that leads to a state system of control—or all repression would have to become automatic. You automatize information and it will say: "Over there, there is a Mafioso stringing up his neighbor, and I send a self-guided dart to punish him, to paralyze him." And then we are off into a sci-fi world and wild imaginings…

Just a moment. Try to compare nuclear deterrence and the system of electronic and computerized repression as we can picture it or imagine it today.

Nuclear deterrence works, if it does, because you burn your own boats. One says: "Excuse me; you are threatening us in such a way that I prefer dying and taking you down with me." De Gaulle said to Kruschev: "We shall die together, Mister Secretary General." So once you get to that point, you can start talking politics. The common threat of a major explosion leads to a preference for negotiation. That is why the Cold War was a constant negotiation. You take Czechoslovakia, alright, we're going to do what we want in Yugoslavia, or elsewhere. The war never happened because there was a common interest that was symbolized and latently fulfilled in the nuclear explosion that could not have been measured.

Paul Virilio called this "state terrorism" when civil populations are held hostage by means of reciprocal threats.

And then it changed a bit near the end when precision weapons began to appear that allowed one to envisage the possibility of ultra-rapid operations that were highly efficient but not nuclear. Now, nuclear arms are no longer a deterrent because there is no more East-West opposition and we are in the detailist era. Yet in spite of everything, you could say that if the United States does not want to wear itself out, which really is the primary part of imperial pre-occupations, and I think that they have them—we can't control everything, we can't dominate everyone, etc.—then I think that Kissinger was being facetious. He said it, but as a way of saying: "See what I mean, they're crazy." Because he is someone who is slightly more capable of considering diplomacy as an art and not a science. And that is where we are: he is more of a European to a certain extent, for better or worse. He is the one who said at the beginning of the Gulf War, but always with a touch of humor, that in any case the decision to start a war instead of an embargo was necessarily made when a certain number of soldiers had been reached and they had to be moved around—because you cannot leave soldiers in the desert with low Coca-Cola supplies for too long, they have to go in shifts—and you cannot move them around without reducing their numbers. There were too many of them to relieve them all in equal amounts without draining all the NATO troops. So they had to use them before withdrawing them because otherwise it would seem like a retreat, and then their leverage would have disappeared. That is a detailed strategy. And then he said that as soon as twenty thousand more men were sent or fifty thousand more, they could not pull out because they had to be used before a given date. Afterwards, they would have had to be withdrawn without using them and the embargo would not have been credible.

And all that despite the aerial forces, the high-precision weaponry, etc.

Yes, because the United States had in some way to create an interest *sui generis* in the success of this military expedition. They could have made it the success of a military presence if they hadn't sent so many men, but since they did, they were forced to use them because otherwise they would have had to withdraw some for no reason.

And the threat itself was not enough? Because it was real.

The threat would have been sufficient if it had remained constant. But if you accept to reduce the contingent before using it…

Yes, but the contingent was only one of the many factors involved in the Gulf: there were also warships, the air strike forces…

If we are reasoning in terms of deterrence, that does not work. There is something psychological involved. If you send an expeditionary force and you reduce its numbers without obtaining anything, your naval blockade loses credibility as well. Moreover, a naval blockade has never been very effective. They find ways around it, especially since Iraq is not even an island, there are holes everywhere. Psychologically, the idea that he would say: "Alright, they are too strong, we will negotiate"—that idea could not occur if the blockade was maintained alone with a contingent that would continue to grow smaller. But informational and technological deterrence is also psychological…

Then they didn't have a choice. They had to attack immediately.

No, as soon as you know that on a given day you have to reduce the number of troops, you have to attack *before*. And that is exactly what happened. And Kissinger said it in September, in other words before it was theoretically decided to attack.

Returning to the notion of deterrence: in order to have a deterrence that replaces nuclear deterrence, first there has to be an adversary; then there has to be a real danger. And there has to be some room for strategy…

It is common these days to study deterrence using the tools Tom Shelling forged under the term "coercion." Shelling is a game and nuclear strategy theorist, but he also conceived of the post-nuclear or para-nuclear starting with the Vietnam War. When the bombing started in Vietnam, everyone thought that the message of these bombings, limited but targeted, would force the Vietnamese to think and say, "OK, under these conditions we will negotiate." That is "coercion" thinking, in other words a pressure that is sufficiently well done to obtain precise results. It did not work in Vietnam, maybe because the North Vietnamese were Communists. Now that there are no more Communists, this pressure should work—and above all, they did not have this electronic time, progress has been made since then—but there was a return to Shelling's thought. These schemas are rational from a certain point of view, from the point of view of strategy on the scale of universal history, but this does not hide the fact that it did not work. Now they think that maybe it could work since the atom is no longer part of the game, because precision electronics, etc., have been improved, satellite observation can observe details down to the metric level, so we should see a system as perfect as Bentham's Panopticon being established, or more what we could call "Panopolitics"... This system is a dream, and dreams are not reality.

But does it constitute a system of deterrence?

Personally, I don't think so at all. Why? Deterrence from something means having an undertaking that corresponds to an ambition, a relationship of forces, etc. But what will be important in considering deterrence is the deterrence of the people.

Which people?

All peoples in general. In the Third World, those who are stuck in the polarized society between accelerated poverty and accelerated wealth. The entire economic strategy will have to be revisited if you want to deter people from revolting. How can you keep people from rising up if they are dying of hunger? Deterrence strategy cannot solve that, they will die, that's all, but they will not have been defeated. You can only defeat the living. Obviously, you can destroy an entire people, but if you do, you cannot call it a victory. If a victory has no goal, it simply ends up being a massacre, though I do not think that is the aim of American civilization and culture. It becomes the objective by accident, in a way, because of the extraordinary increases in precision for targeting and electronics, so in part due to general technological progress. And it becomes the objective because there are no designated enemies, and thus the enemies who remain cannot be named. So they look for a name, a name like "narcotics traffickers," or Islam—but this is not even sure to work, since the Americans work very closely with the Saudi Wahabites. Not Islam, then, but the enemy cannot quite be found. If we look at what we are trying to get rid of: disorder, disturbance. Well, this disorder and these disturbances are caused in part by American economic strategies. The reasoning does not quite bite its tail, and I think that the United States is capable of examining it closer.

But can you find a military form, or shape the military, without having an enemy? Isn't that a bit of a vicious circle? I think it is the current problem.

It is a vicious circle, but you can move around the vicious circle, and one sees how: if you launch humanitarian expeditions to save widows and orphans, little children whose arms are cut off, etc., then there will be expeditions, and the particularly atrocious things going on in Liberia, in Sierra Leone certainly have to be stopped. And yet the cause is not really located in these countries, but in the fact that there have been no efforts made to develop them. If people are dying of hunger, they are ready to do anything; they can take control of a diamond mine. Since a formal state does not exist and redistribution is replaced by corruption... These are all political problems. If you do not have a political program, you let these things continue as Americans are doing. They say: the situation is regrettable, but we are not imperialists. Then the state is not given a shape; only the economy is given a form, a destructive form. If we had some political programs, we would have to approach the problem of social Republics, something the Americans do not do. The only person who opposes the Republic to the Empire there is Patrick Buchanan—he opposes what he calls the "Republic," speaking of the Republican extremist right-wing, to the Democratic Empire, which is not at all what I want to talk about. Buchanan is part of that American tradition that sees the United States as a country blessed by the gods, you find there everything you need, so there is no reason to open up to global commerce or depend on it, etc. This dream has been erased in practice for so many years that Americans do not realize that they survive thanks to forms of commerce that offer them credit, and so they think that they do not need anyone else. If there are so many tragedies now, it is precisely because instead of remaining a normal nation they wanted to rule the world.

The imperial idea is: Laissez faire. Democracy promoted through the economy.

Yes, the President of the United States has a dual role: preside over the United States and dominate the world. That dual function has been around for quite some time.

There is nonetheless a certain shaping on the economic level, since the economy now rules everything. To the extent that it produces democracy, it is thought to be capable of eliminating conflict, etc.

But shaping the economy induces shaping a certain repression. Until now, this repression did not reveal itself overtly as repression because it took the form of state crises and Balkanization...

But elsewhere...

Of course, the United States gets along fine because it has the pipe flowing in its direction, but elsewhere... And repression also appears in the form of the restoration of democracy. Restoring democracy is better than dictatorship in the end. So the free-market economy undergoes a number of transitions in order to coincide with the restoration of democracy, as happened, for example, in Brazil and in Argentina. But this is not the rule. It happens in some countries because they have a history that fits the model that is presented as general. In fact this model is particular to certain countries. Now you have the restoration of democracy in Chile at the same time as a form of crisis that may devalue democracy, even though it is a profoundly democratic country. In Colombia, however, they might have a chance in that they are facing both the harshest economic deregulation measures and the harshest phase of war. So that when things start going better economically, in five or ten years, and democracy and peace are restored, then it will work. That strategy is extremely cruel. It might be an unspoken part of the American system. When we look at it from a European perspective as a historical fact, we seem like the bad guys to American public opinion, which is utterly lacking in historical perspective. In France, we have committed mistakes of this type, as in Algeria. If we had restored democracy at the same time as we introduced the Constantine plan, okay. But we had established the Constantine plan and it did not work and on top of that democracy was not allowed...

In Algeria it was "pacification" with economic measures in tow.

That's right. The idea that we pacified first and then we have a development plan. But the development plan was a plan, therefore a liberal sin. Maybe the Americans will tell us: because you wanted a controlled economy, whereas what we do is liberalism. Just looking at Algeria today, it has been subjected to liberalism without democracy, and it is not clear, the violence unleashed over there, unfortunately. It's rather a dictatorship plus armed groups. And then there is petroleum involved, so we know the American interest is real. I think that in Europe we tend to make up fewer stories, even though we speak less. Americans make nice speeches, pretty radical ones at times. American NGOs are highly critical of the way in which the American government acts, but on the decision-making level of the government, they are not taken into account. NGOs are active, but they have not kept war from breaking out in Colombia. So I think the problem is to have a greater awareness of the relation between the global economic system and the military system. Because the military system in fact cannot resolve the problems of the economic system. It cannot, and all its refinements will never allow it to deal with things on a sufficient level of prevention...

And on the level of the threats…

They involve people who, in any case, are already threatened with so many things that the threat of American military intervention means nothing. At the very least, the Americans will come with sugar and rice, and so the problem does not lie there. I do not know how to define it, but it can only be approached through this question: what is the relationship in the dominant system between the economy and armed violence? Even if you put politics aside, you have to ask that question. Since politics is put aside, the relationship is direct, so let's deal with it. But then everyone will cry out no, that there are different branches of power in the United States, "checks and balances"—so let's deal with the "checks and balances" between the Pentagon and the International Monetary Fund. If the question is absurd because in reality the relationship is mediated by the President of the United States, then there is politics involved. Naturally, the same thing needs to be done for Europe, because in Europe, there is no head, so it is easy, it only depends on the states. There is no head of Europe, and headless money; it isn't credible—that is why it has dropped in value. If a president were ever elected in Europe, the Euro would rise. And it is also true that the United States, as a purely economic or purely military enterprise, has no truth.

There is also a state called the United States, which on top of that is united, something the Europeans are not. That is exactly the opposite situation of what a French Communist writer, André Wurmser, in the 50s, called "The Dis-United States," stigmatizing the divisions in the United States between races, social classes, etc.

It is called the European Union. It will be called "United Europe" when it has the right to have that name, when it is a federal or even confederate state, and then it will be written like the United States in French. Europe has imitated the American process, consciously, since its construction. What was Monnet? He was an American idealist. He said that Europe had to be unified to have the weight of an American-type project. They did their best to unite the European states while in the United States restoring autonomy to the different states is sometimes discussed. It is surely possible that in fifty years, there might be a United Europe that resembles the United States and a United States that resembles a United Europe, but in any case, the United States will lose their monopoly, that of the existence of a single power dominating the central core entirely. *But they will lose this monopoly.* There is no reason to let ourselves keep being fleeced like that...

They will lose this monopoly to the advantage of Europeans?

Yes, to the advantage of Europeans at first. It is inevitable. The European elite is largely the same as the American elite, the number of inhabitants as well, capital rates, etc. And a number of real indexes are stronger in Europe but cannot be seen because of European disunion. So American predominance is inexplicable. In the end, the only obvious and major superiority is military, in other words, the superiority in unification, which includes military unification and the military superiority of the United States, which is in part the fruit of this unification. They only have one army and wanted to rule the world instead of the USSR, so their army remains far superior to all others.

But the army itself, its technological breakthroughs, are in large part due to the economic system they encouraged, and that worked to their benefit.

Yes, technological breakthroughs indeed feed military superiority, but it is impossible to keep them totally within boundaries, and moreover, it is not clear whether this technological military domination is at all useful for dominating a truly over-developed country. Of course, if you can aim and wipe out guys getting worked up, waving sticks and growing poppies in the heart of Pakistan, that is one thing. But to continue to dominate Europe, it may be in the Americans' best interest to maintain a zone of disorder in the vicinity of Europe.

That is what you sometimes suggest.

I am not the only one. And if they had that idea, we would have to make sure they are not tempted to apply it. They might want to maintain a zone of disorder in Russia. It is harder for Europe to control these kinds of things and in fact, such a situation would be catastrophic both for Europe and for the United States. But this problem is not quite leading the agenda, although dominance of Europe through military superiority will not last long, and this for two reasons: the first being that American military means are not quite adapted to dominating allied countries like Europe, which has no more enemies in any case. The second is that purely military domination of an economic system is contrary to American doctrine, to the ideology of peace through commerce, to neo-liberalism, to so-called democratic thought, etc. This thought leads to fascism. And when Americans realize this one day…

Why does it lead to fascism? One could be dominant without using one's force.

Because controlling an economic system through military domination is the definition of a system—one they do not have, by the way—of a system of direct conquest that enslaves inferior populations.

They want the Empire without all the responsibilities.

Right. They have to invent a form of Empire that is not military domination.

And that would be the "shaping."

Yes, they are trying to conceive of shaping as something that will come in part from military superiority, but above all from a feature of what Aristotle called *chrematistics* and also from the economy. Aristotle distinguished carefully between the two, but not the Americans. "Chrematistics" is the speculative bubble, speculation, when money produces money, which, as Aristotle states, is not "natural." Whereas the economy is when work produces resources that allow a house to be well regulated, which is natural according to Aristotelian categories. So if chrematistics and the economy are mixed together, the formation cannot happen.

But that is part of the capitalist system.

It depends on the period.

There was a great period of speculation not too long ago.

Yes, but stimulating a capitalist system also means real investments in the real economy. There is a debate about this, certainly, because there is a speculative bubble that sometimes bursts. It is not an excessive danger and does not call into question the real value of companies in terms of the work invested, which is practically a Marxist definition of Capital, by the way. But it produces social disturbances.

And technology multiplies this even more.

Technology today allows all different types of things to happen, including liquidating markets. The capitalist market is wild in essence, but it is only founded as a pacific object by giving up on its presumptive monopoly of violence, at least on the marketplace. So all that merits further reflection. I think the protests in Seattle set a precedent for us to prevent the advent of a generalized Third World situation, at least in dominant countries. This could be called selfish. No one wants parts of the United States or of Europe to resemble Sierra Leone. But that being said, measures must be taken to prevent the pauperization of the masses from becoming dangerous. So zones of close emigration have to be dealt with.

Mexico, Algeria, South America…

Now there is a substantial American tradition advocating the destruction of pre-capitalist oligarchies, for example. But they did not go far enough, because if the Colombian pre-capitalist oligarchies had been eliminated, then the elections would not have turned out as they are now. Colombia is a country that had an extraordinary capability to switch from oligarchies to capitalist democracy.

The agrarian oligarchies were not eliminated and the Mafia oligarchies set up shop within their structures, along with the extremely violent and criminal practice of *limpieza social*, or social cleansing.

That is even truer of Guatemala.

Guatemala was a total colonial structure that formed a system. In Colombia, it could only be called a colonial structure in terms of a frontier. It is closer to the United States or to Argentina with its enormous space, strong resources, very organized people, entrepreneurs who took part in the clearing and developing the land on their own. It was called the first democracy, yes, but it was also a pioneer zone of land clearing with autonomous entrepreneur farmers, who were incredibly courageous and intelligent people. They are now being killed, and they hide in the cities because they became narcotics dealers. They fled so far away, chased by the latifundiary ambitions of landowners, that they were too isolated to survive from any crop other than marijuana or poppies. These two crops are still the only agricultural products that can be exported by plane without losing money. The drugs are sent to the United States, which denounces the narcotic turn of oligarchic Colombian society, but the peasant farmers are obviously the ones who make the least money. The place where the most money is made is between the Colombian coast and Miami. The wholesalers cut themselves the largest slice. After that benefits diminish down to the smallest dealers.

Returning to the main question: during the first period of deterrence, there was a "blessed moment" when the United States was the only country to possess atomic power. It seems that the U.S. might be trying to return to that blessed moment again. Could they recreate it, or could they possibly regain absolute domination through technology?

It was a blessed moment, indeed, because they had an absolute weapon. Now there are no more absolute weapons. Nuclear power still exists, but it was an absolute weapon for an absolute enemy…

It was an absolute weapon for deterrence. Can technology, the grand technological surge, be used for the same purpose?

I do not think there is any absolute weapon concerned with details. Nuclear power could never become a relative weapon used for precise social objectives precisely because of the enormity of its explosion. Such is its specificity: the incredible forces unleashed by nuclear fission. And we have no software equivalent of such terrifying things. A weapon is hardware. Maximum hardware. Now we have increasingly refined software. So in my opinion, there is no comparison…

Yes, but they're trying their best to keep others from having it.

That is not quite true. The basic fact of commerce is that chips will be made wherever they are cheapest to produce. Suddenly the Pentagon chips are being manufactured in India and probably China. It is very hard to maintain the rationality of profits, of mass production, and this is not limited to military products. One might perfectly well say that there was a unique duel during the United States-Russia nuclear opposition, when all at once two major powers declared themselves to be fundamental enemies, the one fighting for capitalism and the other for Communism, each brandishing the absolute weapon. I don't think that experience will ever happen again.

The absolute weapon is now for relative uses, for the "rogue states," terrorists, etc.

Nuclear weapons have disappeared from strategy. They could only reappear if China declared itself the absolute enemy of the United States. But knowing the Chinese, I think they will be clever enough not to do so. Even if they are, it is best not to say it.

And then they are being subverted from the inside. Because to resist the capitalist system they have to reintroduce it within the Communist nomenclatura.

Yes, they could have slowly turned into a modern fascist regime. But they are gnawed by American-style democracy. No, I think that is over, it will never happen again. I imagine that in ancient history there are culminating points in the opposition between Empires that took place in not so bright and shining centuries. The opposition between the Sassanian and Roman Empires entered into equilibrium and the time when the Romans could have conquered Parthian land was over. Alexander had done it, but he did not conquer Gaul and the Western Mediterranean basin, so one cannot do everything. Worse yet: points of equilibrium cannot be retrieved. If there was a point of equilibrium for the total conquest of Europe, it has come and gone. It was not unthinkable if the Americans had had a conquering-type philosophy, but they were convinced that they did not wish to conquer anything, except the mastery of the world. There is no awareness of conquest. The Americans did not realize that they had *conquered* Germany and Japan, which is why they gave them democracy...

The Germans realized it.

Yes, of course. But they agreed to the process that purged them of the Hitlers and helped them rebuild their nation from scratch. They were not able to do so with a revolution, so they managed to turn out democratic thanks to the Americans. This was not the case for the French, but it was for Germany, and also Japan to a certain extent.

The Japanese recreated à la carte *feudal traditions to hold everything together.*

Because they were not conquered. The Germans were. They were conquered by the Russo-Americans, by the arrival of occupation troops and the total elimination of all political power. The fact that there was an armistice means that a conquest took place and that the German state completely disappeared. This did not happen to the Japanese because they were not defeated. They surrendered after the atomic bomb, but to conquer using an atomic bomb and without using ground forces, there must have been negotiations with the Mikado. So it's over, the Japanese were not really defeated and therefore their democracy is perhaps weaker than German democracy.

That is probably why they refused to recognize the different forms of violence they engaged in at the time.

They have not recognized anything. They were not helped, that is true. When the Americans say then that they never wanted to conquer but to impose a regime, it is all very relative. There are those two examples, which are not negligible. But if they had taken things to their conclusion… They could have conquered France, but de Gaulle stopped them. They had sent orders to take control of the prefectures. But the orders of the French Liberation Committee to send Emissaries of the Republic preceded them and with the people backing them, the Americans could do nothing. They also tried to eliminate French financial autonomy by creating a currency bearing the word "France," if you remember —small bills with the French flag, but not the French Republic, since it was not a Republic. But things were cleared up, I'm not sure how. That is the Gaullist memory. But it was close.

We might all be speaking English now.

The English acted properly. I have incredible memories of the war, in Algeria, since I was in Algeria. My father was a Gaullist and prepared the American landing in North Africa—but then the Americans wanted to have Giraud arrest the Gaullists, so the most threatened went underground. And Capitant, leader of the Gaullist network "Combat," came in secret, protected by a British Army officer from Giraud and the Americans, to visit my father in the house where we were living. Churchill hated de Gaulle, they had heated disputes, but he never went back on his word as a gentleman to help liberate France. He might have wanted Joan of Arc to come from England for once, I don't know. That is why, in France, some people are wary of Americans, not Americans in general, but of a certain type of American incompetence. They are not competent to rule the world. Which is a point in their favor, you will agree…

And that may be why they do not attempt to do it directly…

Yes, but then it should not be called domination. They still want to call it domination, "leadership," with themselves as the leaders. And that is possible for a certain time, in certain places, but not always and everywhere.

Sometimes they recognize this. Sometimes they admit that strategic thinking is not the strongpoint of the United States.

They always recognize everything. It is not the United States, but the American establishment, the system that works. Clinton, who was a man on the left with an internal program, was kept from carrying out his plan. He was pushed to look outside the country to find something that would keep the American working class from disaster. That was his social democratic duty in a way, but it is always the same story: Johnson in Vietnam, the "Great Society"…

Clinton and the "New Economy"…

It was the "New Economy," but we know it was a bubble. Vietnam was a sort of militaristic bubble as well. It kept the factories going, etc. That sounds like propaganda, but I know that I visited the Pentagon when McNamara came to power and McNamara's boys explained it. They gave very clear, very American explanations: the only part of the economy that is legitimately planned now can no longer be the Tennessee Valley Authority, the water, it is industry, and the arms industry because in the arms industry you can say: "Here's what you have to do." It is for defense and is therefore accepted. And that is how jobs can be created. The Pentagon is American social interventionism.

Now they no longer need intervention since weaponry is technology and technology is civilian just as much as it is military.

Which is why there is a real crisis in fact. There was this sort of military Keynesianism that was established and lasted until

Reagan. Reagan did his own Keynesian stimulation through military spending, because Reagan's hypocrisy was to say the worst things about Socialism and to increase the arms credits, which was not much different than what McNamara had done.

In the meantime, the Pentagon spread technology—so that the whole country became militarized without even realizing it.

Technology is civilian in origin as well, and that worries the Americans the most. All of a sudden, they realized that military products were inferior to the non-military production of the New Technology. You need software, you need smart geeks who understand that the progress of computers is like that of type-writers, but even more so. It turned out that military computers were behind the office computers of the civilian sector. That was the discovery of the 1980s.

So they abolished the distinction between the two at that point?

No, but they admitted that the military could look to industrial models for strategic models.

It goes both ways. The Internet, after all, was a military invention—Arpanet...

Yes, it was a military idea. It is not that they were ahead of their times, they thought it was just another device, but then it became a social phenomenon. They were outdone by the levels of tech-nology and office management software. Then they resolved that the army should not fall behind industry, and began to take lessons from industry. That was a small revolution. That was the

"Revolution in Military Affairs" as well. The Revolution in Military Affairs cannot fall behind the business revolution.

In the end, the Americans are training a large part of the population to be virtual soldiers.

Yes, in the sense that soldiers are also keyboard users. But the important theoretical problem lies in the fact that they establish direct contact between military criteria and business criteria, saying that it is not contradictory, except that it bypasses politicians. There is no derivation through politics. And politicians cannot restore a role for themselves even by intervening in trade legislation, where they are very active, obviously under the threat of death—in particular in the narcotics trade, in money laundering—by imposing "good governance," and setting all those types of things as punishable by law. That is its monopoly in a sense. The Pentagon does not want that, and neither does business, although… Because otherwise the Pentagon is threatened by the sovereignty of business. Politicians are running the risk of extinction, even in the United States. They are on the look out. They became absolutely savage with Microsoft in order to see whether they still had the power to intervene in economic morality, in the economy. So they said that it was an old thing, the law, etc… but it is in fact very important since that is where the minimal state intervenes in the economy.

They want no state rival.

They have state rivals, but here it is a trans-state rival, and for absolutely strategic reasons. On the European side, people are aware of this as well. They consider that they have to build something that is equivalent in weight to an American multinational corporation. The government is not the only one saying that, companies do as well. There are effects of concentration carried out in the name of purely economic logic. Even the concentrations of the arms sector follow a corporate logic. But corporate logic is also the logic of the profession and therefore one has to get along with the corporations. And in fact, all the concentrations that have taken place in the high technology and military domains were done by European corporations amongst each other. It was not an order. It was not a political victory, it was not governments who said: "We have to keep multinationals controlled by Americans from forming." Not at all. Everyone thought that there would be "joint ventures," exchanges with American groups, and none ever took place. It is a very interesting mystery.

And what does it reveal?

It means that European corporations seek out European corporations because they have something in common with them, which is corporate culture and *their* version of state regulation. If they ended up with American corporations coming from a different universe, they would not be able to get along, even in terms of profits. As a result, even private companies have a political stance, not a democratic one in any case, but there is a sort of political culture, if you can call corporate culture a political culture. It is nonetheless a way of using people, finding agreements, etc. It is a hierarchical culture, but it has its political side. And it remains mysterious because we can talk about it, but we do not have the concepts to deal with it seriously. Because it is not economics, it is not strategy, it is not politics, we do not know what it is since it does not come from the state either.

In any case it is derived from the weakening of the state.

Yes. But it's a sort of tautology. Because it is power as well. What is this power? I think that the idea needs to be circulated, because it is not really widespread, that we are in the process of killing democratic sovereignty for the sake of corporate sovereignty. Because sovereignty can only exist in states, but if they are only blowing hot air, since the corporations control the real implications, then democracy is ruined. And if you admit that it becomes a form of non-democratic sovereignty, then it is clearer than saying we have to fight with the unions. The unions can do nothing, the proof being that they are pulverized. Or transnational unions are needed.

Attac represents in France a moment of rather interesting awareness; it is apparently grassroots, but it still is strategic. Strategy is that too: identifying interests, people, implications, the shape of formations of alliances and hostilities and in which areas the combats are taking place. One thing I regret, because I will soon have had enough of thinking, and I would like to change my style of writing or cultivate my garden, I regret not being ten years younger. I would like to have ten years more to see where things go.

But it won't stop.

There is a truly extraordinary mutation taking place on the level of capitalism alone; and capitalism does not encompass everything. Marxism remains a trans-disciplinary approach capable of determining strategic problems though incapable of solving them. Yet Marxist categories have to be used to some extent, simply because they are not at all more Marxist than anything else. But we have a tendency to avoid speaking of social classes. You know, the class concept was created by conscientious capitalists, Adam Smith and others, who to my knowledge were not very Marxist. Social class is therefore tied to a conception of the state, which should be peaceful, by the way. Class struggles have to be moderated within states by political systems. So if you get rid of all that, you still don't get rid of the notion of social classes. You get rid of the notion of regulation. It is not because you say: "Ah, now there are only wars between ethnic groups, etc., that is the truth." Ethnic wars are class wars, and one day this will become clear. In my opinion, only ten to fifteen years from now, no more.

And then we will return to classes?

No, we will return to the idea that a notion of class needs to be recreated if we want to take care of each side of human survival: peace, by the protection of the state's monopoly on violence, food survival through the control of means. All this requires democracy, but in regulated circumscriptions. If you no longer have the form of the nation-state, then you need the form of large confederation. Some kind of form is necessary in order for politics to make its objective the avoidance of civil wars—in other words wars between classes. For otherwise, there will be civil wars everywhere.

Paris, May 2001

2. The Empire Strikes Back

Asymmetrical Threats □ Neo-Liberalism and Military Regression □ The "Axis of Evil" □ The Enron Scandal □ Shifting Military Credits □ A Disproportionate Response □ Corporate Sovereignty and the Military Corporation □ The Empire is Taking Shape □ Huntington's Reactionary Scenario □ Hardt and Negri's *Empire* □ From High to Low

In the 2002 State of the Union address, President Bush expanded his "doctrine" to include hostile states: Iraq, Iran and North Korea, the so-called "Axis of Evil." It hadn't taken long for the current administration to put the vicious attack on the World Trade Center to good use and unleash the threat of death over the world. First came the punitive expedition in Afghanistan meant to dismantle the Al Qaeda terrorist network and topple the Taliban regime. Now Iraq is explicitly being targeted. September 11 took everyone by surprise, but the responses were ready. Already two years ago I attended a post-Cold War meeting of military strategists in Cesarea, Israel— it included the chiefs of staff of a dozen countries, including the Pentagon, and specialists in defense—whose main topic was how to respond to "asymmetrical" threats...

Yes, you could say that the Americans had been preparing in a certain way, in an abstract way, since 1995. Clintonian ideology was an act of faith in democracy and in free trade, an extension of liberal economy in ways that weren't exactly liberal— they could even be called tyrannical—but somewhat progressive. One of the thought patterns of globalization considers that everything can be gained by infiltrating the networks of "rogue states." Bush's State of the Union address did not have the same form. On the contrary, it was a general declaration of war against "hostile nations" and terrorism, which is not an adversary. This method used by the strong to fight the weak has always existed, and here it means that the entire military apparatus will be used to attack the weak. Clinton, who is a somewhat neo-liberal democrat, did not take the same position. Of course, the military apparatus he used, when necessary, to articulate threats and launch expeditions, but his goal, the essential definition of his empire, was not reflected in the positions of the American extreme right. The difference between the two is in the manifestation of the use of military violence to fight Evil. Clinton did not display a theological mythology in that way. And that is why Bush has entered into a sort of resonance with the Israeli right, and not just any right, but the religious right founded on an autistic definition of external relations that considers Eretz Israel to be a country threatened with invasion for the past thirty years. So this kind of vision, a purely military, but also theological vision, is something new. There's a kind of Israelization of the United States that goes together with an Americanization of Israel.

It is a major political shift, or a mutation, not only in relation to Israel, but also to the rest of the world.

Yes, it was a mutation in the sense that it engaged both an imperial and a military vision. It implied the existence of two types of enemies: the first, terrorism, is elusive and can therefore appear anywhere; and the second is embodied in state structures. Bush had a strange way of describing these states from the perspective of global diplomatic history, since Iraq is already receiving permanent punishment, while Clinton considered Iran and North Korea to be places where progress could be made.

As soon as the Bush team took office, though, and even before the World Trade Center attack, they moved quickly to isolate North Korea and turn Iraq and Iran into recognizable enemies in order to set the military machine in motion.

Yes, I think there was a very clear decision made by Rumsfeld and the people around him to militarize their global presence by questioning the survival of states that could be called enemies, as well as with "cultures" (as Clinton used the term) which are declared to be "other." Clinton was considering Korean reunification, in other words the liberation of North Korea, after a series of more or less manipulative and menacing preparatory stages. It was a vision of progressive re-conquest based on the model of German reunification: the fatal erosion of North Korea using market forces and the various ways that exist to undermine a tyrannical state using freedom. In the ideology of Anthony Lake or Clinton, there was the idea that they could reach a point where you wouldn't need to use violence if the conspiracy between violent networks and violent states could be averted. Anthony Lake gave a clear definition of this maneuver in some of his speeches. For him, things were not that bad; obviously, there were all sorts of dangers, perils, etc., but fundamentally, there was space for what could be called diplomacy, or rather for manipulating the system, shaping the world by preventing conspiracies from developing between violent states and violent networks. Now, there is more of a confrontation with these two dimensions.

In neo-liberal terms, this appears to be some kind of regression. The Empire strikes back...

This way of calling them tyrannies is in keeping with fantasies of science fiction—they are the mad scientists. That is why, from a European perspective, we have the impression of a regression in diplomatic culture, which mainly consisted in using skill to avoid using force. We have the impression that the decision of President Bush's team aims to emphasize military violence in every case in order to avoid using skill. The question that now must be asked is what sort of future this formula has because it refuses inter-action with constitutive political powers. From the European perspective, the situation in the Mediterranean is a question of proximity that must be negotiated in order to become an act of peace. But if, on the contrary, the American vision is to designate here, there or elsewhere pockets that are considered absolutely dangerous and must be wiped out militarily, then no space is left for maneuvering. Clinton had an offensive vision of the Empire, but it didn't rely on the military, rather on clever maneuvers to go around obstacles and impose norms. The idea was to bring the conquered countries to administrate themselves, which is a definition of liberal empires. With Bush, on the contrary, it is the military that leads the offensive and this changes something in global culture. As soon as you are bent on punishing those who misbehave, there's no more maneuvering. Clinton and his team had a subtler way of bringing the reunification of Korea, of encouraging moderates in Iran. But if you crack down hard on Islam, there is less room for Islamic moderates. Then there is no end to it. Iraq was chosen by Bush senior for the purpose of demonstration and deterrence: if you are not more pliable, this is what will happen to you. But threatening the entire world with Iraq's fate is pretty stupid from the point of view of British imperialism. This is bound to bring together all kinds of people who don't usually get along and force them to prevent this power from asserting its absolute dominance.

Bush answered fanaticism with fanaticism, or paranoia. At worst it's conspiracy theory; at best a risky maneuver.

It is a Manichean, religious, and militaristic regression and we have to ask ourselves what that means. I don't think this vision of the universe corresponds to any reality. Saying that there is an immense terrorist network that is a constant menace for all time is more an ideological vision (or a pathological vision) than one of police. If it is a network, then a police attitude is called for. But if it is a global organization of evil, then we are in a fantasy perception of the international system. And we should justly be worried, because when a political power makes decisions that imply that we believe in that sort of formula, no one can know what will happen next. No formula can really provide a complete response for the universe. I think there was a great deal of surprise, of shock. Europe is not powerless, it is just mute because it has no spokesperson, there is no president of Europe, and no State of the Union address. The State of the Union has become a state of the world. A message concerning the state of the union is a right; a message on the state of the world is not a right, it has been usurped by the President of the United States. Naturally, this is not only problematic from an intellectual point of view, in other words as a well-thought out diagnosis, it is also a program for the world, and a contentious one at that.

It was a two-prong program. The immediate effect of the attack on the United States was to change completely the relationships between the government and the political parties and impose on the population a war-time psychosis justifying the limitations placed on the information concerning military operations, claiming extraordinary rights for the treatment of prisoners and exercising intellectual censorship as well. Few in the United States dared suggest the obvious: that the Bush administration exploited the situation to fulfill its extremist agenda. Those who did were completely shut out from the major media outlets. They could criticize all they want, they wouldn't be heard. Debates were circumscribed very precisely, and some obvious questions were not asked. This was something completely new for the United States, or at least so blatant and extensive.

The event could have been exploited in a thousand different ways, but they decided to take advantage of it in that way. Why? The answer is the regime. The constitution, the functioning of the American state may be in a much deeper crisis than we think and therefore needs mystification to maintain the legitimacy or the power or the effectiveness of its institutions.

The recent Enron scandal could implicate the entire government and it was not entirely by chance that Bush took this very moment to announce an expansion of this doctrine. I wouldn't be surprised if Enron, in the long run, turned out to be far more traumatic to the American population than September 11.

In a functioning regime, scandals lead to failure in elections. There are scandals in France as well, and we will see how politicians involved in possible scandals will perform in elections. But Enron is not only a personal scandal, a mode of corruption. It is a challenge to what I call corporate sovereignty. I have enough confidence in a certain American democracy to think that this fantastical direction will not work. When the Russians invaded half of Europe with all sorts of threats, it was not a fantasy, so public opinion could be mobilized. Even McCarthyism, for all its condemnable excesses, was something like a justification in a real relationship of forces. Now, there is absolutely nothing like that. Korea cannot destroy the world, neither can Iraq or Iran. All that is just a joke. There was no reasonable way of considering this a dangerous situation.

The obvious answer is the huge shift in the military budget. Before September 11, Bush was pushing for a new "Star Wars" effort, overruling the objections of allied powers. Bin Laden provided a far better argument for the Congress to approve the largest increase in defense spending in two decades, as Bush himself boasted.

A 15% increase in the military budget means a Keynesian kick-start for military spending. Democrats are usually the ones to do that; Ronald Reagan himself did the same while saying he was not. Maybe it was a way to jump-start the economy that does not rely on speculation but on state spending. If so, it would become understandable. It would be aimed at providing "good administration," one that we can, of course, criticize, but which is a normal, Machiavellian administration of the American state apparatus. It would claim to be ultra-liberal, but that would just be for the outside. Inside the country, it decided to make a big budgetary effort for redistribution using military credits. This would not be the first time. It would be a response. But you get the impression that something else is involved. Because in order to obtain these military credits, Bush has to create a worldwide danger equivalent to what the USSR could have been. Then the rest of the world begins to think: stop exaggerating. There is no such danger that would justify these war efforts.

Besides Pearl Harbor, the United States has never been attacked before. One could claim that Bush's extreme response and the massive support he got from the population were in large part due to that.

Yes, that can seem like a real thing. It can be mentally reconstructed. Being bombarded is a new experience for Americans. But they are the only ones who can see this experience as new. France was razed when liberated by the Americans. Japan was razed to be occupied. All nations have destruction in their history. The rest of the world has already experienced something like that and its compassion, though real, cannot be infinite. It is not as alarming as a World War prepared by Hitler or the Russians.

The main result, though, has been the overwhelming nationalist response of the American population. Now Bush seems to have free rein to pursue military operations throughout the world. There lies the problem. He seems to be free to do practically anything he wants both inside and outside the United States. It's an unheard-of, frightening situation.

But that is precisely where we want some explanations. It's not because something is unheard-of that it is uncontrollable. It may be unheard-of to receive two Cruise missiles in the Twin Towers, but it is also completely normal given the evolution of technology: there are people who can organize something of that sort. That is why I say the response has been disproportionate. I have had a hard time thinking that it could be as serious as it appears, just as I have a hard time thinking that Israelis are that united. Mass opinions are always appearances. Of course, to a certain extent, massive opinions exist, but then they dissolve, move away.

The Enron affair may well end up being Bush's undoing. External threat could work for a while, but that the most powerful and most trustworthy of all American corporations could not only have folded, but deceived for years the entire financial world, will prove to be the strongest threat for the American population. This was the first time the Bush administration has been called into question, and it resulted from an internal economic event.

I agree. I think that a more surprising phenomenon, something that has nothing to do with terrorism, is the evolution of mergers that have made companies more powerful than most states. These companies have developed a form of sovereignty that allows them to be autonomous, making their own laws and existing with delinquent norms. Delinquent companies are ones that become sovereign to a certain extent. There will be more and more of them. And since you cannot declare war on them—everyone within them is compromised given the fact that the delinquency is located at the level of company administrators and they manage the interests of their stockholders as a form of speculation, etc.—these things cannot be controlled. The only state that is as powerful as a very large corporation is the United States because the machine has other means of resistance. In the United States, the President can speak to the president of a giant multinational corporation as an equal. It doesn't scare him. But taking power back is a different question. It can only be done through the only sizeable state corporation: the military. At least, that is one of the hypotheses I think of when considering the danger of falling into a series of scandals not only in the United States, but everywhere. They are the result of globalization and the rise of corporate sovereignty produced by absolute neo-liberalism. But no one thought it would go so far. One way of reacting might be to require the Pentagon to control 15 billion in credits and manage part of the world violence by turning the mechanisms of police and violent repression towards a re-normalization of financial practices. I do not think that is the way things are going now, but that could have been another version…

To a certain extent, what is happening is a panicked, but also very deliberate, attempt to use the September 11 events to impose American power—and not just American economy—over the rest of the world. After all, the Bush doctrine is a military shaping of economic relationships.

Yes, I think it is an attempt. The most troubling aspect for me is that the shaping is purely American. You meet Americans these days that say: 'Europe? We don't give a damn about Europe!' You can very well not give damn about Europe, and Europe cannot give a damn about the US, but this is not a glorious point of view. When you start asking questions about interactions, you also start examining such an "idiotic" vision, in the etymological sense of the word—autistic, singular, something that cannot be shared. Americans cannot share their massing of public opinion: it is a singular experience. But the fact that they do not care to convince the rest of the world is something rare. It is the end of alliances, first of all, and even if it is not, it will mark allied relationships. Which means something is not working in the Atlantic community.

Let's not forget that the United States itself is undergoing globalization. It does it as the top dog, of course, but this ultimately translates into a limitation in state power of America as well. Couldn't we say that the stark military escalation we're now witnessing is an attempt to assert American leadership even at the expense of traditional alliances? Earlier on we discussed the fact that the United States had not yet found its shape. I wonder if the events of September 11 have not led to defining it. The American Empire that did not quite exist before may in fact be taking shape before our very eyes.

I agree with you completely. The Empire is taking shape right now. It has been slowly forming since 1995-96 and has resulted in a much more military form than was predicted. Under Clinton, there were other ways of presenting things. The opposition between Anthony Lake and Samuel Huntington at least was a schema for reordering things. Huntington appeared as a reactionary and pessimistic ideologist who gave an image of the world that ended up defining geographic, militarized fault lines according to cultural differences, which was his way to transcribe the end of the inter-state logic needed in an empire. Then, in its place, things were constructed to determine large cultural spaces, but some things were sacrificed. Huntington practically said that you couldn't do anything with the Arabs, or with the Orthodox Greeks, because they are Orientals. This kind of machinery seemed a little improbable to me, but now something of that nature is occurring along with an increase in military presence that is not directed at cultures precisely. And yet if you look closely at the situation, there are only Muslims and those Huntington calls Tao Confucians. So the Japanese better sit tight and the Chinese as well. There is an extension dating back to 1996 that has now reached the entire world, except India and China. Everywhere else, there are military commanders with "areas of responsibility" over central Asia; over the Caucasus and Siberia. Other than that, what is left? India and China remain outside American control because the Pacific Command, PACOM, is a naval one; it only covers the coasts up to Madagascar. So if we take seriously the fact that these are zones of eventual projective force, an exterior is taking shape that includes India and China at present. India is a grand civilization, but it cannot be called a competitive religion, so it is closed off. China is not quite in the same situation. And Islam is condemned, or it is on the frontier, they do not want it to exist as such. They can always try to sell this kind of Huntingtonian scenario to the Europeans, but they won't succeed.

I don't think they tried either.

There is a deliberate absence of attempts to establish contact. I find that very disturbing. Sharon is doing the same thing in a way. It is as if the United States and Israel have synchronized their approach, because they have decided to close themselves off, saying that they are on the defensive. Whence the debate about whether to enclose Jerusalem with a wall or to surround the Palestinian villages with walls. In any case, they need ghettos, so better it be someone else who is put in them. These are truly dramatic problems, but they also mean the end of liberalism.

Talking of liberalism, have you read Empire *by Toni Negri and Michael Hardt? The idea there is that America is not the Empire but at most a form that represents it. The Empire itself has now reached a global level and accepts no limits or fixed boundaries. It's deterritorialization on the widest scale. Contrary to Gilles Deleuze and*

Félix Guattari, they believe that this globality can only be answered in kind. No more molecular revolutions or specificities. Empire meets counter-Empire. Would you agree with this analysis?

I do not think they have taken the military question seriously enough. They have a somewhat idealistic vision, perhaps even a Clintonian vision, of the expansion of the capitalist system. What we are seeing now calls into doubt not the veracity, but the capacity Negri has to represent the Empire in question.

We talked about the Empire, but it was an Empire with various strategies to maintain an authority that could not be absolute; that did not want to be absolute or even direct. This is precisely what is being called into question. But what we are seeing at present might not be a symptom of strength but rather of weakness. It is an attempt to regain the absolute Empire that never was, and make it American...

Yes, but it looks like a transition from a High to a Low Empire.

New York-Paris, May 2002

I

INTRODUCTION: CHAOS TODAY

It is in the interest of the person who wages war by choice and ambition to conquer and preserve what is conquered. He acts to enrich both his country and the one conquered instead of impoverishing it.
—Machiavelli.[2]

People sometimes ask me about the state of the world, and more often how to deal with its changes or rather the violence of its changes. They want to see a full-color map, or better yet be offered a high-resolution, animated overview of the landscape. What they need is a shaman and not a scientist for such a task since it is more literary, or even magical, than scientific. The world today is united by a new form of chaos, an imperial chaos, dominated by the *imperium* of the United States, though not controlled by it. We lack the words to describe this new system, while being surrounded by its images.

Geopolitics

Of course we do have geopolitics, a literary vision based on a few resilient facts, the geographical hard facts observed from above. But movements? predictions? prevention? prophecy? The major concepts of geopolitics are shaped by the fear and will to dominate of the Germans and the English, some "wishful thinking" guided by a *Schadenfreude,* simplified nationalist teachings that even children could understand. But it is no more ridiculous than any other representation. In fact, each and every one of us demonstrates the ability to survey future horizons around the dinner table, or over a cup of coffee; no one would deny it, since the desire for representations is part of being human, man or woman, with a curious mix of curiosity and hope, just as it was for Pandora.

But it is an art more than a science. The polemology that both pacifists and fundamentalist militarists desire does not exist. There is no general crisis model that could control the unexpected with threats or promises formulated in advance using the memory of scenarios of a possible future.

Why not then approach the problem from the point of view of a different shaman, one who does not agree with those who consider the present evolution of the world as leading to electronic fascism, an irrevocable *brave new world* that should *therefore* make us rejoice? Philosophy, as the desire to attain wisdom, continually offers questions (indefinitely) rather than providing answers (definitively). "Socrates," Hannah Arendt once wrote, "is a lover of perplexity."[3] I should therefore be able to propose a philosophical geopolitics while peppering my shaman's vision with questions, questions to which history will provide the answers. If we ask the right questions, and if we put up a good fight, history will take the form that we have suggested.

I will therefore question the shape of the world that the strategic leadership of the United States imposed on Europe and the rest of the planet, and confront it with other futures. Is the American Empire primarily economical or military? What form of power will prove capable of controlling and opposing what, in the present leadership of the world, is leading us to a catastrophe? In order to raise this question, I will first revisit the foundations of the state, from Republic to Empire, as they have been shaped in the West from Machiavelli to Hobbes and Clausewitz. It is through the function of *protection*, in economic terms as well, that the state legitimizes the monopoly of armed force and fends off the "war of everyone against everyone," this state of nature that came to a stop at the end of the Middle Ages. We're presently sliding back into it, and this includes fanaticized fervor politicized by abusive clergies within the three religions of the Book. Little wars, endless and cruel, are erupting everywhere since the Gulf War announced the end of the bipolar era. In spite of their power, the United States is not willing to conquer the world in order to ensure order and peace. It doesn't intend to assume the general protection of citizens, only regulate disorder through norms of behavior implanted in their allies. This strategy of avoidance, shirking socio-economical responsibilities, has become spectacular with the challenge raised by the terrorist attack led by Bin Laden and the punitive response in Afghanistan. The impasse which Sharon's strategy imposes on Israeli-Palestinian relations and the return to wars of colonization are part and parcel of this imperial school.

I must, however, provide concrete objects for this perplexity as well as a general goal. My general goal is to understand wars in order to work towards peace. I will therefore begin with the description of chaos today.

As for the objects, although considering all the cases of *wars taking the shape of "frozen peace processes"* that can be found throughout the world, I have chosen to concentrate on four processes: the two Balkan wars in Bosnia and Kosovo, the Latin American war in Colombia and the Arab-Israeli war in Palestine. I am not trying to provide exhaustive descriptive monographs on these recent conflicts but rather rework the questions poorly formulated in the chronicles of the time that contributed to the moral and political dissatisfaction and uneasiness in democratic and leftist opinions, especially in Europe.

My choice is not purely theoretical either. I have not excluded the war-peaces in Africa and Asia for any defensible reason; the tragedies they involve will be mentioned whenever possible, although it seems impossible for me to provide accurate reasoning about countries that I have not studied in the "field." I have traveled up and down the Balkans and Latin America for years. I have also visited the Middle East, both the Arab world and Israel, as well as the Mediterranean Basin, which gave birth to the illumination of the world and carries with it the grand street and café-terrace culture, the secret power of oppressed women, the source of Greek, Arab, Italian, Spanish and French genius. But during these trips, I discovered that all the theology surrounding strategic debates since Plato was put under tight surveillance starting in the 17th century by an English political philosophy that aimed at escaping imperfection with the support of the people rather than creating a perfect regime with the help of God, or by relying on absolute intellectual awakening.

With these precautions in mind, a certain modesty is necessary in approaching the frightening problem of the multiplication of savage contemporary wars that *accompanies* the rise of an overwhelming world imperial power. This power, which refuses *to conquer* the world, only seeks to fill its own pockets. We are confronted with a global power that takes infinitely varied local forms while refusing to *think* of local variety except in terms of temporal uniformity; and it succeeds thanks to its ability to establish norms, not to conquer. It is now trying to sustain this unconquered empire by shirking the requirements that Machiavelli outlined: *the obligation to enrich the conquered peoples as much as the conquerors.*

America and Europe

We must cast our eyes on the New World, if that is the area with the dominant project today, in order to penetrate the genetic code behind its strength. In a manner of speaking, however, since this is just a biological parable. It serves to remind us of the fact that we are confronted, no doubt, with a living being, the North American state, albeit a political creature, a conglomerate of citizens. How and why can the *law* that has guided the autonomous development of American power since the discovery of the New World by Christopher Columbus be understood and pronounced?

Invaded in the north by Anglo-Saxon Protestants from Northern Europe, in the south by Spanish and Portuguese Catholics from Southern Europe, the two parts of America provide two different examples of genocide.

The genocide of Indians was almost total in North America and the slave trade became the project behind the southern United States; the Indian genocide in the South was interrupted by the *encomienda* that inaugurated a personal regime resembling the colonies of the Low Empire with vice-kingdoms that took over the Inca and Aztec Empires, and slavery was tempered by the ritualized and generalized emancipatory miscegenation that triumphed in South America along with the Spanish and Portuguese languages. Then, in the two autonomous new worlds founded by Washington and Bolivar, the North slowly but surely overtook the South, to such an extent that the New World as a whole described the potential image of the North-South relationship in the entire world.

In Europe, Orthodox Christianity and Islam, as continuations of antique culture, were immobilized in antique conquering structures and slowly underwent the humiliating fate of economically inferior countries corrupted by the petroleum windfall along with the venal and police bureaucracies that are politically kept outside democratic European culture. Europe has a South on its eastern and southern flanks, but this South is already, due to the economic and military constraints that weigh on it, under American control.

The future of Europe would therefore be as an associate dominant zone, condemned by its divisions to submit to the visible center of world military and economic power located in the United States. Europe and its historic citizenship would resemble the Greek city-states under the Roman Empire: the Greek source of Roman culture fell under the control of Rome in 197 BC when the consul Flaminius declared "the freedoms of the Hellens restored." His proclamation prophesied their subservience when Rome banished "forever" the preeminence of the Macedonians and other Middle Eastern peoples over Mediterranean cities in favor of the Roman imperium,[4] in much the same way that the United States liberated Europe from the German Empire and the Soviet Empire, proclaiming the freedom of the historic democracies of Europe, in exchange for their submission to NATO.

To critique and perhaps alter this evolution of humanity, the chaotic strategic configuration that currently defines the American Empire must be taken as a whole, while considering its foundations, even if it is necessary to remain attached to reality through local investigations and anecdotes.

Which will entail the persistent analysis of *confrontations*.

In any case, no matter the scale at which the object—continent, nation, neighborhood, family—is situated, we must always ask whether the war we are faced with is a war of Balkanization, the destruction of a type of political cooperation, or a war of Liberation, the destruction of a mode of oppression.

When the two types of processes are superimposed or cumulative due to *scalar* effects, political debate, which defines objectives of intervention and third-party participation, themes of peace research, must be refined as much as possible according to confirmed political goals, and certainly not in the name of "maintaining order" since it is a question of disorder.

Our contact with chaos must not become a chance for parties on either side to depoliticize cynically or grossly simplify its implications as a result of intellectual laziness or misinformation, as can be seen in the many examples over the past few years in the Balkans, the Mediterranean or the Caribbean.

Moreover, the analysis of wars in terms of dominant class and new or old popular class interests must not be abandoned. Cruel internal wars financed by Mafias and with paramilitary armies have developed in many regions of the world since the end of the Cold War, in forms and for reasons that, by definition, can no longer be connected to the global bipolar dialectic between the capitalists and the Communists, even if they first broke out within this ideological framework. During the bipolar period, all conflicts were reduced to class conflicts. Today, we should not commit the opposite error of seeing only bandits and intercommunity conflicts everywhere.

State Decomposition and Globalization

These cruel little wars have spread over the ruins of the system of Communist federal nation-states (Yugoslavia, Russia), in non-Communist nation-states once in full free market capitalist expansion "through import substitution" (Colombia) and in national states formed by single party, non-Communist revolutions / liberations (PRI Mexico, Kemalist Turkey, FLN Algeria).

During the various processes of state decomposition, armed conflict between linguistic, religious or Mafia communities (and usually all three simultaneously) creates combat systems that legitimize long-term strategies of assassination, kidnapping or territorial cleansing involving more or less sadistic massacres provoking mass exodus (Serbia, Colombia, Algeria). In Sub-Saharan Africa, the crises of post-colonial states have degenerated into conflicts between communities across borders: Sudan, Rwanda, Burundi, Zaire for Central Africa; Guinea, Sierra Leone, Liberia for West Africa. In Indonesia, the decomposition of the vast island federation, a legacy of the Dutch East Indies Empire, might only have begun.

We might ask whether these Balkanizations are not also "national liberations" or, on the contrary reductions to "protectorate status," or even slow processes of reunification of linguistic nationalities, long sacrificed and divided by imperial frontiers or prior Balkanizations (Kurds, Albanians, Basques, Irish). Even if the combats have sometimes, literally, taken the form of "ethnic" wars, the fact remains that they originate in oppositions between the interests of ruling classes seeking to take power by dividing the popular classes by means of massacres between "ethnic groups," then joining them locally under ruling class hegemony by creating "security zones" on a smaller scale along the lines of state decomposition.

The wide variety of "identity cases" leading to violence and war should not occult the fact that all these cases can now be combined and explained by a common, and not at all secondary, factor: the grand macroeconomic process of economic globalization following the computer revolution.

The general effect of globalization, its most general strategic definition, could be stated as follows: *the disjunction of political, military and economic criteria once coordinated by the state at the geographic level of the state*. This disjunction constitutes the common source of diverse individual cases, allowing us to understand the proliferation of common symptoms, notably the outbreaks of cruelty and savagery, despite the cultural, historical and sociological differences that distinguish each of these suffering societies.

It is very important to preserve a global anthropological approach to each of these cases, for it allows their common traits, and their causes, to become more apparent. These wars cannot be attributed to the "barbarity" of one ethnic group or religion but always to the intolerable suffering that accompanies the destruction of former solidarity by ruling Mafias and the great difficulty in creating new solidarity with the risk of falling into the "fraternity of war crimes."

In all the spaces where composite, multi-ethnic federal societies of conviviality have been destroyed or have self-destructed, their inhabitants preserve a melancholic and embellished memory of their prior civilization, or at least of the values it tried to represent, or in which it attempted to believe. The Soviet Union, Yugoslavia under Tito, multicultural Bosnia all joined the Austro-Hungarian Empire in the paradise of the past.

In memory of these disjointed hopes, the analysis of conjoining destruction today must maintain a large-scale project for peace and reject the blunt, day-by-day myopic realism of the sordid accountants of other people's misery. The contemptuous post- or neo-colonial mindset displayed by mediocre leaders often hastens these crises towards the worst catastrophes, which they follow with a sort of *Schadenfreude*, a neo-Darwinian pleasure in watching others suffer close to an "unconscious fascism" valid for the exterior.

Wars of Balkanization and liberation become "current" and not "archaic" when they are put in the context of the processes of market economy globalization and the unification of the "chaotic" imperial system known as the American Empire.

This presentation will also allow me to describe the necessary characteristics of the peace processes that can be opposed to them and guide the European school of peace along different paths than those proposed by the American school. We all know perfectly well that there are partisans of the American school in Europe and defenders of the European school in America, but I will use these names for the sake of convenience. The American school assumes globalization as a smoothing over of all political territories as non-sovereignties (except the territory of the United States). The European school on the other hand looks to cover the globalized economic world with sovereign socio-historical political identities.

No "Domino Effect"

Here we must venture what might seem to be a contradictory judgement: the danger of these little wars for world peace is negligible, for even if global macroeconomic factors are deter-minant, their implications and specific causes are, by definition, local in nature. They actually take place *within the historical and geographical framework of the states in crisis* and their evolution depends on the specific political decomposition that the indi-vidual states undergo.

Contrary to the famous domino theory, these conflicts do not really tend to contaminate their neighbors and cross borders, except perhaps in Africa where the post-colonial borders for states without long historical consolidation cut through the tribal, linguistic and ethnic groups that form living identities.

Elsewhere, "contamination" does not work, even in the Middle East and in Northern Africa, despite the unity of the Arab language and the preeminence of Islam, neither in the

Middle East nor in Latin America, despite the unity of the Spanish language and the preeminence of Catholicism. This non-contamination can no doubt be explained by the constant attempts of the imperial system to maintain a certain order while reinforcing divisions; but it must also be noted that the nation-states, even within the process of destruction, retain the form of semi-sealed compartments; the effect of the mosaic structure *opposes* a generalized crisis in the states of a subcontinent. A state in crisis "holds in place" through the resistance of its neighbors, or the states of a given region simply maintain their identity because of the substantial socio-political differences between their respective national crises. Their differences counteract the spread of *social* movements across frontiers.

Wherever a cross-border *ethnic* movement can join populations combined prior to the formation of a colonial or post-colonial state, the United States tends to favor minority indigenous peoples, which is a way to Balkanize and limit political class struggle. However, the choice of the political left by Indian movements in Latin America (in Mexico, Ecuador, Peru and Chili), like the Kabyle movement in Algeria, have made them one of the unifying components of anti-imperialist, anti-globalist thought. Even if by definition they cannot become majority movements, they are symbols of liberation.

In the context of the Latin American narco-economy, the United States, under Clinton, claimed to fear "contamination"— a reincarnation of the "domino theory"—in many of its official statements; truth be told, the United States might have wanted it to occur. America does not exist as a decision maker, it is rather a permanent debate. By this name, I am only designating the result of the play of forces in competition.

In fact, abroad and at home, the trans-state factor of the

"narco-economy" unifies states around a police-military task, and thanks to this activity across borders, the United States spares itself the element that serves federal or imperial hegemony in the state: the minimal justice-police state. Abroad, it is possible, with or without democracy, and thanks to the narco-economy and the fight against narcotics trafficking, to unify "minimum states" *militarily* faster than by unifying the economic elite through generalized dollarization, and much more safely than by supporting an ideological Indianism, that could always end up turning into a social Indianism, as happened with Chavez or *sub-comandante* Marcos.

Political Civil Wars

If current "narco" states took harder individual stances to solve this problem, there are chances that they would have to strengthen their sovereignty, including economic sovereignty, to confront the problems at a social and political level; however, national management of the narcotics problem would slow neoliberal globalization.

For all these reasons, Post-Cold War America sponsors a few of the "peace processes" that emerge from zones of massacre, called "violence," but their theoretical approach to crisis intervention lacks conceptual clarity; the moral or religious principles that they defend keep them from recognizing the contradictions between the strategies they set out to implement. Barbaric war appears to involve only minuscule territories along with an *apartheid* or clan, region, Religious or neighborhood war dialectic that have little to do with the splendid "globalization" unfurling over the planet. These wars seem to involve delinquent groups serving corrupted politicians. This is not incorrect, but it reduces political collapse to a form of delinquency[5] while this delinquency itself should be considered a particular form of political collapse.

Finally, the virtual decision-maker sometimes preserves its ability to erase the macropolitical causes of all these disturbances from the public mind by only assigning them micro-sociological causes like the growth of assassins' guilds, cartels, ordinary generalized corruption, bank accounts in Miami, Switzerland or Cyprus on the criminal or penal level. Maintaining the secrecy of these acts has been made more difficult today thanks to the action of highly specialized NGOs like *Amnesty International*, the *International Human Rights Federation*, and even *Doctors of the World* or *Doctors without Borders* which always relate the crimes of a nation in crisis to its political, social and economic context.

In this sense, all of these wars are truly political civil wars, even if they are skillfully diverted by the new ruling classes into conflicts apparently waged between communities that are capable of eliminating through bloodshed, in other words "concretely," the interests of the diverse social classes defined as trans-ethnic.

Binary and Ternary Conflicts

Our strategic approach to the study of violence obliges us to note that a certain number of these little chaotic disorders are formally bipolar and go back to the Cold War, imitating its bipolarity down to the smallest details—by building walls, dividing cities and countrysides—but more often than not without representing the same goals: capitalism versus Communism.

Binary conflicts occur most frequently between communities where one "religious nationality" is pitted against another (Arab Muslims against Jews in Palestine, Orthodox Greeks against Muslim Turks in Cyprus, Protestants against Catholics in Northern Ireland, Muslims against Hindus in Kashmir). The creation of these new sites of binary confrontations is inseparable from the desire expressed by these conflicting nations and classes *to escape the binary logic of the Cold War*, both its dual leadership and its latent structures of *class* civil war, by proclaiming a local bipolarity between "nations" or religions. It is the international equivalent of confrontation in certain democratic two-party systems. Republicans versus Democrats in the United States, Conservatives versus Liberals in Colombia are not the same as "right versus left," thus allowing political conflict to be distanced from the ambition to incarnate pure social conflict peacefully. Greeks versus Turks is not the equivalent of Communists versus capitalists, allowing them to avoid civil war within each nation and also war, since the two countries are allies within NATO.

Nicaragua, Guatemala, El Salvador, Colombia each harbor binary conflicts inherited from the Cold War and guerilla movements fighting the oligarchy's armies. They continue to represent Cold War polarity. The first three received peaceful *treatment* through a process of negotiations that began as the world was reaching the end of the bipolar context. Colombia is the only local binary struggle that is still paying for the East-West conflict (agrarian reform, welfare state demanded by the guerillas), though without the presence of the former Soviet Union. The agrarian Colombian war takes on added complexity with the financial and transnational factor provided by narco-agriculture. Its exception proves the rule.

Other local conflicts are even more complex and more recently formed. One might say they seem to illustrate the "clash of civilizations" theory proposed by Samuel Huntington. They are engaged in wars between communities that sometimes resemble wars between religions or between religions and the state (Bosnia, Kosovo, Algeria). Often occurring in Post-Ottoman areas, these wars are ethnic as well as religious (Lebanon, Israel-Palestine) or ethno-linguistic (Kurdistan-Kosovo).

Moreover, they often go through periods of complex disorder that could be defined as "three-sided wars." Obviously, this would appear to be the case in areas that already have three religions, as in Bosnia or Lebanon. But religion is probably not the defining factor. The war in Colombia is also ternary even if the three groups—guerillas, army and paramilitary forces—are not separated by a religious membrane.

The Israeli-Palestinian war could become ternary or even quaternary if the religious or class factors took a more open role in the conflict, not only in Israel but on the Palestinian side as well. This might happen soon enough.

There are peace processes that "succeed" after decades of setbacks (Northern Ireland, Cambodia, El Salvador, Guatemala); and others that have yet to begin (Cyprus, Kurdistan, Algeria).

Others systematically fail (Spanish Basque country) by sinking into horror (Rwanda, Zaire, Chechnya).

Still others break down, halted by retractions that reveal the diplomatic failures of American leaders: when the United States succeeds in imposing itself as the sole mediator (Palestine, Bosnia), there is no way to conclude a lasting peace in the brief period allowed by the four-year terms of American presidents, reduced to three years by their election campaigns.

Frozen peace processes are the most revelatory of the state of the entire international system. They last long enough to define themselves as endless conflicts tied to globalization.

Frozen Peace

Not the same as a local failure, a "breakdown" is first and foremost a new product of globalized diplomacy.

Accelerated negotiations coupled with indefinitely postponed implementation (Bosnia, Kosovo, Palestine, Colombia) are combined with the spatio-temporal criteria of American domination and the interplay of leadership divided by the hostility between the Executive and Legislative branches: under Clinton, rapid diplomatic success was required by the 4-year terms of Presidential mandates; codicils signed for only one year by the Republican majority paralyzed or undermined the long-term strategic engagements of the Democratic Executive. The final product: powerlessness or, at best, what American jargon has termed *mission creep*, the slow deformation of the definition of military missions. Quite a few military writings reveal the deep-set professional concern accompanying what we could call the appearance of non-Clausewitzian wars, wars that do not "continue politics or diplomacy by other (violent) means" and are not started, as was the case during the Second World War or the Cold War, in order to restore or establish democracy.[6]

Nevertheless, the absence of common war goals between the UN, the United States and European states should not be taken for a lack of political goals. *War is not "non-Clausewitzian," but the coalitions (internal or external) are incoherent.*

Let us return to this question.

The mission objectives first given to troops wearing light blue or olive green helmets often change form imperceptibly along with the political goals. What seems odd is that, in this situation of disunion or non-cooperation, the deformation of the *Ziel* (the wartime military objective, in Clausewitzian terms) by leading military commanders alters the *Zweck* (the *political* goal of war-peace, in Clausewitzian terms) and not the contrary. This might shock the external allies (states), and may also shock the interior allies (the Congress) of the leader of military power (the President of the United States).

Which means that *in these cases* military operations do not continue politics by other (violent) means.

Since there is no *single* common policy, variable local military tasks can come to influence and modify the vague or contradictory initial political goals. These interventions are therefore not considered "Clausewitzian," which does not prevent Clausewitzian local wars from existing. Their local *goals* are very much political and opposed, but the common *military objective* of the outside participants, with no common political goal, cannot be defined except as a *desire to exercise military control over the war*. Because they take part at a level of autonomy and coherence that is inferior to that of the local warriors—they disagree on the level of conflict with one actor or another—they take time to control the conflict and can only do so through the absolute use of military violence.

For the UN and NATO, this is not a war *at all*, but for the Serbs, Croats and Muslims, it is a war and a Clausewitzian one at that.

Humanitarian Wars

The unbalanced Clausewitzian character of the interventions in cruel little wars is accompanied by a particular perversion: their international treatment through "humanitarian" aid. This humanitarian action can pass for a purely political objective. Of course, humanitarian actions exist for themselves; in the field, they usually precede the expedition of UN soldiers. They are real and political and legally founded and praiseworthy in themselves. The point of perplexity concerns their connection with the classic scenario that makes war "a mere continuation of politics by other means."

The connection between humanitarian aid and war, to a certain extent contrary to nature, contributes to confusing the political meaning of events: by countering the Clausewitzian politics-war "continuation" with an illusory "humanitarian aid-peace" continuation, the true political goals of war (*Zweck*) can be *hidden* while its military operational goals (*Ziel*) are paralyzed.

By using humanitarian aid, war ceases to refer to politics and becomes angelic, in other words disincarnate. The Celestial Blue of the UN or the white background of the Red Cross represent this disincarnation; the presence of military units removing the war from politics while at the same time removing it from armed action simply bears witness to the purity of the humanitarian intentions of the international community in the face of unchecked barbarity.

A great unease weighs on these undertakings since even deaf and mute public opinion can see and understand that expeditionary humanitarian forces are *powerless* to fight barbarity. It turns the world television audience into a Roman plebe of voyeurs, ashamed of being constantly invited to watch the bloody circus games and witness innocent victims being devoured by the lions. The amount of UN soldiers with serious neuroses continues to rise as they are subjected to an unprecedented situation for a soldier, trained to fight an enemy, then stripped of the right to ride off in knightly armor in order to protect the innocent, watching them get ruthlessly slaughtered.

If it were only a question of "pulling the wool" over people's eyes, the situation would be serious from a democratic point of view, but history has often done without democracy in affairs of external violence. It would not be the first time that public opinion has been ignored for a *realpolitik* in exterior spheres that requires deathly silence from the fundamental moral principles of democracy: human rights violations are always accepted *as long as they remain unspoken*. War is the continuation of politics through other means. War crimes are part of a strategy of means and they do not interrupt the rationality of Clausewitzian continuation, taking place on the level of the *Ziel*. Military goals justify military means. *It is not a military affair if the means used to serve a military goal (Ziel) ruin the political goal (Zweck)*. Politicians must judge these actions and be judged by them. Which is why the clean conscience of torturers is protected by the bad conscience of politicians. But we will have to wait thirty years for one of them to have their medals taken away.

Then again, Clausewitzian rationality has been broken and a superior degree of moral perversion has been reached. When humanitarian action accompanies and serves to compensate for, or hide, a *crime against humanity* tolerated by policy, there is not only a breach of morality but of political rationality on both sides, not far from madness. For without political rationality, war is nothing other than madness.

The massacres of civilians and planned genocide that often occurred in ancient and medieval history have not always been contrary to political rationality and, to this extent, they were not considered illegitimate until recently. Some Serb nationalists (or more recently, Israeli nationalists) simply considered themselves to be traditional Machiavellians and Clausewitzians. But in the modern conditions of the economy, genocide and territorial expulsion of an ethnic group do not correspond to a rational objective unless one admits in the absolute that there are too many human beings on the planet. In itself, the genocide organized by the Serbs to purify their territory does not correspond to any reasonable objective in terms of politics or economic development. It clearly led Serbia to lose all political legitimacy and to military defeat. That is why it only took a few years to award General Divjak the Legion of Honor because he served his country, multicultural Bosnia, against the genocidal criminals of the Serbian Republic of Bosnia, supported by the French government. But Europe *allowed* them to continue along this path by only opposing their politics with humanitarian intervention.

Through its proximity to crimes against humanity, "humanitarian war" introduces a maximum level of moral and political confusion. One could say that the humanitarian pretext, when put forward by the Empire, always serves to blur the two Clausewitzian articulations of politics and war, which require democratic political debate when taken separately.

Democratic debate concerning the political goals of war is therefore threatened by the deployment of this humanitarian smokescreen. The "Doctors of the World" association, among other NGOs, has spoken out against the scandal. It has not kept it from intervening in chaotic zones, but has forced it to name political representatives in order to avoid playing the role of a smokescreen for the Empire.

Chaos of Words

In the transitional period that we are now crossing, even political leaders sometimes do not know what they are doing. In other words, *they do not have the words at their disposal to name their powerlessness, or their power,* and therefore their moral or political conscience in the new international system remains clouded. They lack the landmarks necessary to alter their understanding, and therefore to propose a rational policy in relationship to potential goals. It is important for democracy to actively search for the means to *punish the language and words of political leaders*, to invite them to speak about what they are doing, to make them speak the truth. But there are many democratic schools. Or rather many democratic cultures.

Journalists have a prominent role to play in this domain, as do the elected representatives who have access to the media. They can either clarify or obscure public understanding. The efforts for clarity, for clarification are never unanimous; but it must be said, today more than ever, that part of the search for power involves handing the reins to *an empire that reigns through the chaos of words, as much as the chaos of things*.

In order to determine political responsibility and criticize it, one must admit that there has been a latent opposition between American strategy and European strategies, but also a latent opposition between two schools of speaking the truth and two schools of speaking falsehoods, connected to two democratic schools. The involvement of two European schools and two American schools has lead to a great deal of incoherence in the representations that public opinion has had of these wars and in the humanitarian implications that the wars in Yugoslavia overtly expressed. We hope, by untangling these webs, to make things clearer in the future and strengthen the actions that are capable of affecting the political future of the world.

II

THE EMPIRE: ECONOMICAL OR MILITARY?

If the form proposed for the world empire is a chaos, we have the right to believe that it is begging the question of the end of free market capitalism. It is an ancient right. Except for the brief period of militant neoliberal media triumph that we are now traversing, one that started with Thatcher and Reagan, the question of the end of capitalism has not stopped being raised since its rise in the 19th century.

It is tempting in fact to consider the contradiction between "Empire" and "disorder" to be insoluble and to pose the general question of decadence: Why does the world, dominated by the United States, seem to be heading towards a decline, an imperial chaos that resembles, more than anything else, the Low Roman Empire. This recognition seems to presage the end of the current mode of production known as capitalism, just as the Low Roman Empire presaged the end of classical slavery.

The end of capitalism was a question that haunted Marx (who wanted to topple it) as well as Weber (who wanted to save it). These two 19th-century men, just as steeped in classical culture as Machiavelli, sought a method to predict and forge a political future.

Weber looked for a response to this question through the "idealtype" method and historical comparison. He wanted to understand why the Roman Empire arose from a city-state civilization, then collapsed without reaching capitalist accumulation; and why capitalism arose from a new civilization of city-states in the Middle Ages, while conserving and developing free labor. He admitted that the end of the Roman Empire represented the collapse of a *slave economy* that he perfectly defined as an *Idealtyp*.

Weber went farther in this search than Marx by subtly defining the relationship between military violence and economy. He acknowledged that the relationship between free and forced labor, which competed in ancient Greece, shifted with the Roman Empire to a predominance of slavery. "Because people without freedom were inexpensive," he noted, "war took the form of a slave hunt."[7] Weber, like Marx, believed that free labor was the most progressive form: with free labor, in fact, the division of labor—which leads to specialization among workers and therefore progress in techniques—starts by being identified with the growing extension of the market. A market economy and areas of exchange can spread extensively by progressing through space, but can also develop intensively in a single space by including the greatest number of people who had been excluded at first... The urban bourgeoisie (*Bürgerschaft*) sought to destroy aristocratic property by expanding the market both extensively and intensively.

However, in antiquity, in cases of forced labor, "the progression of the division of labor," Weber writes, "developed through the increasing number of people: the more slaves or serfs there were, the more forced tasks could become specialized."

Free labor and exchange declined in the classical period because people were inexpensive and people were inexpensive because wars had all the characteristics of slave hunts "...which put free labor *at the stage of salaried work without capital*" (*auf des Stufe der besitzlosen Kunden Lohnarbeit*). Technical progress through division of forced labor broke down due to the lack of a free market. In the Middle Ages, on the other hand, free labor and exchanges increased and free activity developed through salaried work and accumulation of capital.

The military organization of violence therefore determined the dominant mode of production and not the contrary, in any case in the two modes of non-capitalist production, because violence alone (or perhaps violence plus religion) can organize forced labor—almost a tautology. The defeat of slavery was necessary for capital to be accumulated.

But what about today?

Applying this "Marxo-Weberian" method to the analysis of the present-day situation leads us to propose the following :

Today, there is a form of servitude in all Third World factories that weighs on the free labor of prosperous countries. People without freedom are inexpensive. But they can't be had without waging a slave-gathering war by depreciating agricultural knowledge, destroying country life, increasing influx to urban centers and turning the masses of agrarian popular classes into delinquent plebes. The accumulation of free workers without work has now been disconnected from the division of labor and progress. Progress occurs by introducing new technology and electronic equipment into machines, and the division of labor is a division of machine labor. So free people are worth as much as slaves as they are as workers. From a moral and profit-based perspective, they can be massacred, not in order to conquer them or reduce them to slavery, but just to subdue them.

Why? How? For whose benefit? For how much longer?

This Chaos is recent.

1. Genesis of the Empire

There was once, in the past century, the 20th, a "free world" and a "Communist world," each obeying its laws, its images, its lies and its idols, and a "Third World" which attempted to separate itself from the two others thanks to its size and despite its weakness. When the tripartite world of bipolar nuclear stand-off seemed to disappear with the end of the Cold War, it was believed that the earth would finally become peaceful, or at least conform to the order outlined in the UN charter. This belief buoyed the courage and conscience of the nations allied against the Iraqi dictator after his invasion of Kuwait. But the illusion did not last long. Why?

The World has by definition retained its "shape,"[8] but the UN must bow before the whims of its leader. The United States is determined to shape the world in its own image. It is a world united by a principle of disorder, a world-chaos, which is nothing like an orderly French garden. It took ten years for this project to take shape in the United States and spread across the earth, with its own particular debates, truths, stakes, methods, vocabulary, myths and lies.

A "chaos" has now completely, and for years to come, replaced the orderly world of the Cold War. Nonetheless it has a dynamic morphology: an overdeveloped core, zones forming constellations of democracy or free market clusters in circular form, then, farther away, zones separated by flexible or ephemeral institutional, economic or military membranes; zones in crisis, zones of barbaric violence, social wastelands and slow or rapid genocide; a surveillance system consisting of observational satellites and of bureaucracies to interpret their observations and databases; a non-hierarchical system of communication, telephone, internet, cyberspace, an infosphere structured as an anarchic, but diversified, space. A system of repression as well: mobile or fixed military bases and stockpiles all in coordination to maintain the logistics of global military intervention; systems of alliances and Euro-American command systems under American control.

This structured chaos follows a fractal model. Its zoning appears at every scale: on the global scale, the continental scale, the regional, national and provincial levels, and perhaps even at the level of cities, neighborhoods, families or individuals, since the crisis reaches all levels.

Tell me what your core-fortress is, your social wasteland, your genocide and your logistical means of expeditionary intervention, and I will tell you who you are. Emperor, king, Mafia boss, respected citizen, angry ghetto resident, junkie, madman, suicide victim. This empire of disorder is not a super-state; it imposes itself at every level. How can it be defined?

Global "Nobles" and Slaves

States and their governments were founded on the idea of order and how to "re-establish" it by any means necessary. These organisms have now been stripped of almost all their former political power to shape local society through the transnationalization of capital and multinational conglomerates. In order to hide their current decadence from their constituents, governments continue to act, claiming their regal prerogatives, especially when, through some merciless mechanism, the financial system abandons them.

No matter which party is in power, and especially in wealthy countries where corporate reasoning is even superior to the family, nation states have become, in fact, the rational agents of destruction of their own economic and social sovereignty. Is the so-called modernization of the state suicide? The Fed, GATT, the G7, the OECD, the IMF, the World Bank, Davos, [the World Economic Forum], the EBRD, the EIB, the ECB, all of these institutions that can be considered as technical oligarchic organisms, aim to produce, propose and make each nation incorporate the new juridical instruments of this *diminutio capitis*, which decapitates politics.

This situation poses a serious problem for the democracies created after the anti-monarchical revolutions in England, France and America: by beheading the king (or chasing him away), they aimed to give sovereignty to the people, to the now and forever autonomous citizens, empowered with freedom against the state, equality against the nobility and even fraternity against the clergy. Today, however, the sovereign rule that has been taken away from the nation-states has also been taken from the people and from kings. It has not gone to the "technocrats" either, but rather to the corporations, and within the corporations, for the moment, to the executive directors of the corporations rather than its stockholders, the corporate parliament where one pays for the right to vote. Stockholders may sanction a corporation by selling their holdings and markets by refusing to buy, but the real strategy lies in merger diplomacy, one more secret and spectacular than those employed by kings of yore.

Davos, which journalist culture has not hesitated to call "the meeting of the masters of the world,"[9] now proffers sovereign political speeches ("financial speculation must be controlled by forbidding short term bank loans" announced one corporate leader at Davos in 1998—who wished to remain anonymous). Corporations that have become sovereign transnational organisms are guided in principle by groups of wealthy individuals with no national ties and near-sighted interests, and by banks that according to their statutes obey no one. These two powers have always existed in the modern era, but previously were due to the local combination of financial and industrial interests, under the control and auspices of a sovereign territorial body. This body obliged them to keep their feet on the ground, less by means of threats than through well-understood common interests. Wherein it was said, and rightly so, that the interests of the (geographic) state were no different than those of the ruling class, the "national" bourgeoisies.

However, the corporations and new dominant classes conglomerated in the Empire have become transnational sovereign institutions, now obeying in principle groups of independently wealthy individuals with neither hearth nor home, created by the need for establishing private pension funds with nearsighted interests. They also obey the banks that, statutorily, answer to no one but play a very regulated speculative game by order of corporations and states.

The imperial counter-revolution is the return of the "nobility." This poses a serious problem for the democracies that arose after the anti-monarchical revolutions in England, France or America as well as for all their descendants: by decapitating the sovereign-king (or chasing him out), they attempted to give power to the people, to their citizens who became forever autonomous, capable of freedom against the state, of equality against the nobility and even of fraternity against the clergy. This strategic representation of the state of peace has come under question.

Question 1: Isn't the much discussed economic "globalization" nothing more than a reshaping of the political sphere wherein chaos deprives sovereign peoples of all their local sovereignty while handing it to a sort of old-regime and firmly anti-democratic aristocracy of businessmen? The anger of the "peoples of the world" could turn against it, if a World existed. The World-chaos, however, does not exist as a political entity and the People of the World are merely a "virtual" counterpart to the ruling *Corporations*; the "People of the World" are even more virtual than the "International Proletariat" of old.

Question 2: It is not clear that this chaotic neoconservative order can be eliminated by an immediate counter-offensive from those who are nostalgic for the revolutions of 1649, 1793, 1848, 1871, 1917, 1968. Is it at least possible to slow it down, to hinder its progress, to lead the world towards a more pleasant chaos?

The expansion of the myth of "universal competition" is upheld by the wheeling flank of world power with all the furor and fascination of Nazi or Stalinist propaganda, and it often consists of an assemblage of gross theoretical lies that manipulate popular hope.

Question 3: Can the hope of "finding a stable job and living a happy, though modest life," survive with the *freeing of corporations* from the regulations guaranteeing the application of social agreements? Or, on the contrary, will this situation increase inequality in a completely uncontrolled and inhuman way?

The neoliberal ideology of the global aristocracy is much more "peaceful" than the ideologies of Stalin or Hitler, since it contains no official call for concentration camps or massacres; it does, however, sugarcoat a cruel reality. For a number of years or decades, one could already witness with the naked eye a return to a form of *free-market slavery* in certain Third World countries by fixing salaries at the subsistence level—under the threat of death, with hordes of new labor descending on cities and through the elimination of subsistence farming. Thus, in Brazil, new kinds of urban zones / slave markets have appeared between the departure from Nordeste and arrival in the South. In order to remain competitive with robotic modernization, these subservient workers must become precarious, underpaid and even "disposable," like razors, according to the term invented in Latin America (*deshechables*) for the useless human residue of exploitation and social misery. Drug addicts, prostitutes and street children are rounded up and slaughtered in certain cities by masked brigades of para-police officers. In Colombia, this type of activity was called *limpieza social*, social cleansing, long before the invention of "ethnic cleansing" by the Serbs. "Free market concentration camps," based on the Maquiladoras model of a few towns on the Mexican border, can now be found almost everywhere. Social relations in the production of underdevelopment hang like a threat or presage of the future over employees in wealthy countries. This model is today the explicit inspiration of the only model of development that the Israeli and American extreme right offer the martyred population of Palestine. We now realize that the principle of apartheid, once thought condemned, is as alive as ever. And Mexico is the largest Bantustan of the United States, just as Gaza and the Palestinian parcels in the West Bank are the small Bantustans of little Israel. Can we willfully and antiliberally reverse what appears to be a barbaric regression on a global scale?

Question 4: Isn't a defense still possible, first through an ethical refusal and then by basing resistance on the structure of chaos itself? By reshaping their oligarchic power through control of the electronic chaos, the oligarchs have a head start. Need we believe that the people as a multitude, the nation as a pact, the state as a local reason are incapable of establishing a non-hierarchical, pluralist action against the real and symbolic power of the electronic aristocracies, and even of rallying the electronic middle classes who have not yet acquired the culture of mass assassination?

We maintain the idea that, even with the acentral organization of the world, the fundamental values of democracy, in other words, popular control of power, can regain strength and assert themselves against the fundamental values of the oligarchic dictatorship that now has the wind in its sail.

Europeans *therefore* now have the new task to choose the form of chaos they prefer and try to achieve it by steering away from the form of disorder proposed by "American" leaders. Their leadership can be felt even in the heart of Europe along with their formidable will to power. Democracy, the nation, internationalism, Socialism will have to be reinvented, not by adjusting to cruel and brutal exterior circumstances, not by managing the growing inequality in the world nor by administrating locally the pleasure of being rich or of escaping slaughter, but by attempting to reverse this movement like those who thought they could stop the expansion of Nazism.

Let us admit that in a chaotic world, the free market dominates the exchange of ideas. Today, after the victories for *judicial freedom* and *political equality* in the West, we were supposed to be managing the principle of *social fraternity*—a principle that the Communist regimes had hoped to embody, although with more gulag and less freedom, before their project went bankrupt—which does not mean that the product advertised has been removed from the market, which leads us to a 5th question.

Political Solidarity

Question 5: What is the status of Fraternity in the exchange of Ideas? Shouldn't the end of the *abusive* Soviet monopoly over the production of political fraternity normally lead to opening up the production of more fraternal social systems to competition? The neo-Darwinist, neoliberal project is now advertised as "inevitably producing happiness," but this is false advertising. The market, in other words the people, consumers of just ideas, will soon rid themselves of this dishonest product. Already, some of the "new masters" are worried, and a few are sincerely trying to act like enlightened despots. This is a civilized phenomenon, not a barbaric one. Soros has become a benefactor for the regions sacrificed in the triumph of the savage globalization that made his fortune. Soros is not only a businessman, he is the founding father of an order. Saint Theresa of Avila was not only a mystic who founded an order, she was also a shrewd businesswoman who appropriated the gold of the Conquistadors. Even high echelon bankers make humanist or social proclamations. Citizens of every country, like free electrons, have come together in either recent or long-standing transnational non-governmental organizations with the concrete goal of building fraternity: organizations such as Amnesty International, Doctors of the World and Doctors without Borders, Helsinki Watch, the League of Human Rights. More recently, the UN High Commission on Refugees declared its jurisdiction in internal wars, the ICRC ratified the respect of the Geneva Convention for internal wars... This transnationalization of fraternity has engendered widespread disarray, but can also serve to make international political consciousness progress rapidly.

Thanks to advances in science, robotics and the potential

abundance of resources, the Fraternity mentioned in the French republican slogan (Liberty, Equality, Fraternity) has become possible in theory, but not without a state, and not without politics. Nations and their citizens, however, have already handed over to corporations many of the political components needed to lead the world in the direction laid out by our Enlightenment ancestors.

The most hardened *sovereigntists* will go so far as to accuse NGOs, that work to establish fraternity, of being instruments used to destroy nation-states and steal their monopolies. The people will appreciate the absurdity of this analysis. In the current disorder, it is preferable to organize a sphere of political fraternity *with citizens and without states*, rather than sitting back to watch the victory of the transnational wealthy classes and their smiling neofascism, which calls for *nations without citizens* in order to control the carrot and the stick. Or while the sinister and suicidal neo-fascism of the Salafist oligarchies triumph, former allies of the CIA, in connection to the sumptuous public works projects of the corrupt monarchy reigning over Mecca and Medina. The success of this large-scale *nobilitary reaction* is far enough advanced, through the global expansion of ruthless neo-Darwinism, that these efforts alone have no chance of bringing things back to the way they were before. We must therefore move forward.

Moreover, with the development of new weapons, alliances without enemies are being formed on the transnational scale of the post-Gulf War world, along with repression without casualties and selective genocide supervised from above by empty-headed governments that control professional or even private armies. New mercenaries will be supervised by different communities, or different local armies will be incited to fight against each other, with whole peoples sacrificed in fights to the death like gladiators "to gratify with the sight of battle" the new "Roman people." I have borrowed this expression from Tacitus[10] in his description of the wars between the Germanic tribes that took place north of the Rhine and the Danube, like in a vast amphitheater, without disturbing the frontiers of the Roman Empire. Television, with its live broadcasts of massacres, has become the modern equivalent of the Coliseum if the fascination exercised by the slaughter is greater than the critical commentary.

What *political* mediation remains available to express the principle of fraternity actively on the international level?

A form of disorder compatible with political fraternity it not beyond the reach of the imagination. Nevertheless, Europe should by all intents and purposes be the recipient in which just such a reshaping of possibilities takes place.

In 1995, in France, when both the postal service (*La Poste*) and the train service (*SNCF*) were on strike, it became clear that an attack was being led against the major public services by the private forces of global modernisation. Clear that a struggle was engaged against the slow death of the public service-state. 1995 was also the year of the fall and genocide of Srebrenica; a particularly shameful year for France, Europe, NATO, the United States, for the entire system of the "empire of disorder." In 1996, the strike by truck drivers was a *strike in the workplace*. For a category of workers whose workplace includes the roads and highways of France and Europe, this meant occupying the national territory, the former symbol of sovereignty, and the European territory, the new space of the community. By holding their strike on this logistical crossroads, the French truckers demonstrated the existence of a "logistical fraternity." Spanish truck drivers were furious at first, then followed their example. The strike was very inconvenient for society as a whole, but it remained popular. Why? Truck drivers are the only members of the proletariat whose jobs cannot be "relocated in Thailand." There was an awareness of the possible safeguard of class solidarity at the national and international level of formerly sovereign territories. The intrusion of strike-breaking Mafias of Russian drivers also contributed to the recognition of the unity of logistical space as a political solidarity. As the history of the Teamsters in the United States has shown, drivers' unions are always threatened with Mafia infiltration. This question deserves a theoretical approach.

Finally, in 1997-98, the movement of unemployed workers in France brought with it the awareness of the structural impossibility of eliminating unemployment and the demand for a *political* solution to preserve the social dignity of all citizens when globalizing modernization necessarily creates structural unemployment, putting individuals out of commission and forcing them to social exclusion.

The unemployed in 1998 "merely" wanted article 21 of the Montagnard Declaration of Human Rights of 1793 to be put into action: "Public aid is a sacred debt. Society owes subsistence to unfortunate citizens either by procuring them work or by ensuring that those who are unable to work have the means to exist."

It should be noted that this article 21 both combines and weakens articles 10 and 11 of the declaration of rights drafted by Robespierre (presented on April 24, 1793 to the Convention before the fall of the Girondins). Robespierre spoke of something much more precise: "Society is obliged to guarantee the subsistence *of all its members*, either by procuring them work or by ensuring that those who are unable to work have the means to exist" (art. 10); "Requisite aid for those who lack the necessary means is owed *by those who possess an overabundance.*" (art. 11) The call in article 11 of his project to define aid as a debt of the rich to the poor (rather than fraternal kindness) was removed by the Montagnard convention. The moderate members of the single party began to hold more sway, and not less, after the elimination of the Girondins.

After 205 years, article 11, founded on political rather than on humanitarian rights, was once again a topic of contemporary debate. It does not apply to a period of serious crisis of the means of subsistence, but to the cruise-ship regime of renewed economic growth. It does not apply to the situation of a particular nation-state, but to the critical state of the World Republic, which is under the threat of becoming the World Empire.

The Seattle movement in 1999 as well as Genoa in 2000 were the most recent episode of the awareness we have just outlined and the first of the social movements that occupies this global space. It displayed a demand whose content is very old in a very modern form: the request to annul the debt of the poor.

Debt Cancellation

The Pope is well-aware that this problem is not just a denominational one. He ordained that during the 2000 jubilee year, the annulment of Third World debt was a priority for which he invoked the words of the *Pater Noster*.

Many Catholics were stunned after reading the news. In French—as in Spanish—the text reads: "Pardonnez-nous nos offenses comme nous pardonnons aussi ceux qui nous ont offensés"[11] without any mention of debt cancellation. Why is such a *false translation* used in France, Spain and all Latin America? I did not have time to research the question as fully as it deserves; however, the *Le Monde* newspaper, generally well-informed, found it necessary to explain this sudden appearance of debt in the Lord's Prayer with the slightly embarrassed mention that the *Holy Father was using the Italian version of the Lord's Prayer, which is much closer to the Latin version.* The Holy Father is simply obliged to refer to the Greek version, the only original and canonical one, which states rather bluntly: annul our debts in the same way that we also annul the debts others owe us, after the Greek: (αφες ημιν τα οφειληματα ημων ως και ημεις αφιεμεν τοις οφειλετοις ημων).

In Greek, *aphiêmi* (αφιεμι) means "to drop," "to abandon definitively" and not "to extend the payment deadline." *Opheilêmata* (οφειληματα) refers to debts in the everyday sense. But since God obviously did not lend any money to mankind, and certainly not at a high interest rate, the meaning here is metaphorical—at least for God. To evoke *redemption,* a *divine act,* the only human equivalent would be *the annulment of all debts that the poor owe the rich.* Sound advice for any wealthy person who would imitate God. This act is the only one in the earthly realm that symbolizes a new beginning, a new order *full of hope* and no longer based on the rule of unequal gains (and the force of armed men over unarmed men that springs from unequal chances and the accumulation of wealth), but based on the love or *philia,* or the Holy Ghost present in everyone.

Not many people are aware of the fact that there is no mention of *forgiveness* or *offence* in the Lord's Prayer—except in the French, Spanish and Book of Common Prayer version. Why might that be? Forgiving sins or trespasses refers to ethics, individual psychology, or even penitence after the confession. The annulment of debts invokes a much more revolutionary act of *political* brotherhood, especially on the planetary level where Christianity is supposed to operate. The annulment of debts was moreover at the time of Christ, in both the Greek and Jewish cultures, a specific, intelligent, *common* political gesture for the Jews (the annulment of debts every fifty years during jubilee celebrations), and *rather common* in Greek city-states: an act aimed at preventing civil war and reestablishing harmony between the social classes. In fact, a system in which the gap between rich and poor grew, leading the poor to go deeper into debt or steal in order to survive, led straight to internal slavery or civil war that could destroy the city. It became necessary not only to find the cause of this unrest, deadly for the city-states, but also to eliminate it radically so as to start over on more favorable terms.

Cancellation of debts was a political commonplace in ancient Greek culture, and the same was true for Rome, which politically could be considered a Greek city-state. Rome requested its laws from the Oracle at Delphi. The pulse of the Republic followed the often violent conflicts between plebeians and patricians over the legality of the enslavement of debtors, a procedure that had been abolished in Athens by Solon in 594 BC and was only eliminated in Rome some 268 years later in 326 BC. When the Lord's Prayer took shape in both the Greek and Latin spheres, the annulment of debts for the poor was the best way in the entire Mediterranean arena to provide a *political* representation of what was meant by the will of God, the New Testament of Christianity: redemption is the prerogative of God against spiritual slavery, the end of a restrictive belief in original sin and the proclamation of the liberty, equality and fraternity of all Christians, who were thus *redeemed*, in other words *freed* from slavery, to use the vocabulary of the period.

The French Republic annulled the debts of a part of its population only once in its history: for the veterans of the First World War, and the October Revolution of 1917 played no small part in helping the politicians take such a drastic measures. Lionel Jospin, in 2000, made it a point to restore the civil dignity of those who participated in the mutiny of 1917 against the senseless butchery of the offensives ordered by General Nivelle. It was one way to annul a debt. Not to pardon the offenses. Today, there is a movement to annul a part of the *public* debt of the Third World, but the private debt of these countries remains sacred. The debt of the poor resists all amnesty. The debt of the rich often takes the form of loans guaranteed by capital flight.

We cannot count on the Davos club to push for legislation that would annul this private debt. To hope so would not be very democratic. Already, for Aristotle, *justice produced by a relationship of forces always creates fraternity; fraternity does not create justice*. Having become familiar with such *godforsaken places* as Beirut, Jerusalem, Sarajevo over the years and my own research concerning Colombia, Guatemala, Mexico, Somalia, Rwanda and Algeria, oblige me to start with a diagnosis marked by terror and pain, but also by the resistance of moral forces.

According to Clausewitz, moral force enters into the calculation of political forces at the same level as military force. The beliefs taught by religions, or by any other ethical system certainly is part of power relationships. There is no lack of forces, but their organization must be reconsidered since the pact between peoples and their governments and the new, secret pact between governments and corporations has been broken.

That is why, despite the despicable state of the contemporary world and the principal subject of this work, I persist in seeing it as a study in optimism, one that must be founded on an affirmation of the Republic as protector of a sovereign people. In order to deploy the bouquet of forces in the right place and return to a form of peace, I will start by revisiting the moment when the modern protective state was born.

2. Hobbes, Birth of the Republican Protection

It is impossible that a Commonwealth should stand where no one else but the Sovereign hath a power of giving greater rewards than life, and of inflicting greater punishments than death.
—Leviathan, Chap. XXXVIII

In the absence of a declared enemy, the most formidable enemy one must face in politics is disorder. Chaos comes first; the ordered world is second and always under threat. Disorder is present everywhere, like liberty, and this type of threat is never lacking as long as an elite brings it to the fore. This is the case today, although only because neo-liberal ideology (the "universal language" that has taken over the ideological sphere dominated by corporate presidents) paradoxically considers disorder to be positive and order negative, the equivalent to an abuse of power. Yet the representation of disorder as something harmful was the original source of the political desire for order.

The Divine State against Chaos

For the ancient Egyptians, and perhaps for us as well, "creation did not affect all of the possible. It appeared as an oasis of order in the midst of the threatening Chaos that subsisted around it, and it even carried with it such phenomena as night where the forces of destruction move freely through the ordered world."

For the Egyptians as for the Sumerians, beginnings held great importance, but there was also a wide variety of cosmogonies, the past was open to an infinite variety of beginnings. They did not have a single genesis, but multiple ones; in fact, as many geneses as were necessary to explain the birth of all phenomena. The order of creation from the local organizations in the Nile valley or the Sumerian city-villages did not proceed from the state. On the contrary, the state came from the growing proliferation of the order of creation and only then from centralized rationality. Finally it was the establishment of Pharaoh's power as a sort of god, or the power of the Semitic conquerors of Akkad above the Tigris and Euphrates, or of the mountain and nomadic tribal regions that imposed centrality.

The "memory" of an aggregate of microcosms preceding the centralized cosmos of the state remained in both the Sumerian and Egyptian religions. This "memory" was defined as a system of struggle between two representations of politics and power. The first tended towards the autonomy of productive forces and their concentration under the economic rationality of the temples, their partial predation through the clergy, masters of the silos and legitimized by their regulatory economic function. The other tended to impose the violent needs of a centralized predatory power favoring elites through armed force. The "centralization of the gods," and therefore of economic and political power, could have taken place in two ways in Egypt: through the domination of a local clergy promoting its god, the local god then becoming the sun god, like Amon-Ra; or through the invention of a single god by the central political authority. Like the sun spreading its life-giving rays equally to all men, Aton, created by Amenophis IV, became Akhenaton, and limited the political ambition of Amon's clergy in favor of a divine form of the republic without the clergy. The struggle between these two suns was merciless. Aton was quickly defeated. Egypt and Sumeria did not place the military arts at the heart of their power; they continued to consider the cosmos as the management of a natural and radiant combination of water and earth providing exceptional economic resources, while disorder was located in the destruction of dikes, discord between cities or city-states, violence, obscurity and invasion.

The idea of a single god causing a single beginning of the world by means of a military victory at the summit of a pyramid of subordinate gods, appeared as the dominant administrative representation of empires: the divine-kings reigned over the priests like the chief god ruling the gods, and the warriors dominated the workers condemned to the glebe. Conquerors, obviously, were anxious to rationalize centralized management of the irrigation-drainage, which river civilizations had carefully organized through up- and downstream negotiations. The second definition of order therefore was state violence acting as a parasite on the power of temples and the submission of peasants by means of hydraulic works. This model was reproduced both by the Akkadians, who lifted their god to the summit of the Sumerian-Akkadian Olympus, and by the Assyrians who elevated their god Mardouk. Even outside areas of fluvial culture, the Greeks described Zeus' rise to power over the other gods after his victory over the Titan sons of the Earth. In Rome, after Roman military power overpowered the merchant Greek city-states and the Etruscan hydraulic cities, the triumph of Jupiter (he was placed by Titus on the site of the Temple of Solomon) was the penultimate example of a version of divine and imperial military that Antiquity produced and reproduced over many millennia. Constantine's conversion to Christianity followed by the expansion of Islam under the Sultans, leaders of the faithful, and the unification of Christendom during Crusades, were the ultimate examples of this representation of universal divine states that owe part of their legitimacy to the centrality of war as a creator of peace.

Non-military order and multiple, non-centralized divinities can always appear as disorder. The periods of disturbance that have rhythmed imperial history from Antiquity to the present, obviously were recurrent moments in the cycles of decomposition-recomposition of power. This is the way a very longstanding popular tradition of the biblical religions considered them. Disorder is only a new beginning because it potentially contains a variety of possible orders, a variety of scales of possible orders. Disorder always opens a new choice of degrees of order.

History can be seen as an infinite collection of these minute or enormous beginnings and new beginnings. Sovereignty is established by predatory violence or by means of the economy and the rational management of reserves.

The primary problem of contemporary disorder is that, for the first time perhaps, humanity has embarked on an ocean of disorder with no final order in sight. This disorder does not initiate any order, simply a disorder that begins over and over again. Orders are given to us from on high, from the heights of the major financial institutions. They don't come from the president of the United

States, a monarch with almost no power, but from the headless neo-liberal power. This single giant empire that claims to order everything through disorder is usually called the "market." Of course, we like disorder almost as much as we like order. Disorder is necessary, especially when a fixed principle of order exists to be transgressed, which is almost always the case. But order is always necessary because it provides protection. Obedience is not arbitrary; in any case, it is not solely motivated by terror.

Protection of a Mortal God

From Hobbes to Carl Schmitt, and up to the most recent theoreticians of the electronic American Empire (sometimes close to fascism), the relationship between protection and obedience is said to remain the only explanation of power. "Anyone who does not have the power to protect others does not have the right to require their obedience"; "anyone who does have that power can constantly incite obedience by all effective means that do not always have to be immoral: by guaranteeing protection and a quiet life, by educating, by invoking common interests against other people." Consent creates power but power also creates consent.

This vision seems to define power as a product of obedience. But "old man Hobbes," as Diderot called him, was slyer than Carl Schmitt, for if you look closely at what Hobbes wrote, obedience resulted from the consent of the people organizing their protection as freely as they can. Even if he was convinced that absolute monarchy offered the most perfect protection for the people, he admitted that any form the Commonwealth assumed is made legitimate by the people in terms of protection.

All people—and not just the weak—need civilized order as part of their lives: the need for protection comes before class distinctions and is therefore always produced as well in class societies from classes of age or gender roles. "For [the child] ought to obey him by whom it is preserved, because preservation of life being the end for which one man becomes subject to another, every man is supposed to promise obedience to him in whose power it is to save or destroy him." [*Leviathan*, XX]

Children need order because they need protection due to their initial weakness, and women, due to their maternal roles, and the elderly as well, due to their final weakness, and mature men, since they start to wear down, and youths, due to their rash spontaneity and lack of experience, and finally everyone needs order and protection, not a terrifying order that makes you prefer death to life, but an acceptable order, that makes happiness possible and even gives transgression the sense of a progression.

Feudal men pleaded with their lord to protect his loyal subjects, his devoted vassals, by placing their hands in his. The modern meaning of protection, however, first appears with Hobbes.

Protection is *naturally* the only legitimate function of sovereignty, it begins with the relationship between parents and their children. Yet, according to Hobbes, it is not provided *politically* by a supreme savior, but by what he calls "the multitude united in a single person," or "a mortal god to whom we owe our peace and protection," in other words, "an artificial man." The recipient of this artificial personality is known as the *Sovereign*: this is the *great Leviathan*, the biblical creature Hobbes assimilates with the state, with the Republic. Hobbes translates the word *res publica*— word for word the "public thing" in Latin—as *common-wealth* in English. He clearly states that this Sovereign can be the people as a whole, an elected assembly, or a monarch. Hobbes favors absolute monarchy as the form of sovereignty, but does not allow his own preferences to cloud the scientific development of his theory of power.

We must therefore reread Hobbes, before Locke and Montesquieu and Rousseau, for the modern consciousness of the sovereign state began with his thought in the mid-17th century. Over the past 250 years everything has changed, but not enough to have rendered the essential ideas of the "Republic" completely absurd, even if they continue to evolve.

The notion that *the Republic is born as an idea with Hobbes* is, of course, up for discussion. By selecting this particular strategic moment, I want to show that the Republic cannot be born without a *revolution* and that Hobbes, through his method of analysis, also considered a crisis involving the entire state as the most fertile moment for a theory of power. By revolution, I mean a type of mass popular movement that braves death out of love for the common good, during which deep-set popular convictions are expressed and make possible the desire to renew society, the state and happiness. This renewal can take place as a return to origins or as an innovation, but in either case it uses archetypal representations of the political imagination, like Liberty, Equality and Fraternity, which have been revered separately (or together) since ancient times.

Those who have lived through such circumstances know that a revolutionary process is characterized by the brilliant intelligence and passionate enthusiasm of the agents who "spring from the people," the immediate emergence of new thoughts and new talents. Like them or not, revolutions are definite historical objects, although they lack sufficient theorization (too many social sciences must be mobilized to do so). No one tries to theorize during a revolution because everyone is far too occupied elsewhere. Afterwards it is often too late. The moments are too *fleeting*, either because the revolution "succeeds," or because it is "suppressed," or "recuperated"; the end result quickly seems so commonplace that any study appears to take this end result—the new institutions, new laws, new ethics that triumph or suppression have stabilized—as its point of departure, whereas the richness of a revolution resides in its heady rational improvisation. Lawmakers and social observers follow. But even without a theory of movement, the revolutionary moment is necessary, from what I have been able to gather, for the creation of the Republics of our modern and contemporary periods.

We must return to the moment when the representation of the Republic first emerged, as well as its separation from feudal disorder *and* from absolute monarchy. Reading Hobbes, we can develop a number of certainties concerning what should be maintained in today's Republic (in the French sense of a popular sovereignty following a royal decapitation by Jacobins) as a source for imagining the future and as a reality of the contemporary world. Not that the *essence* of the Republic will be found at the end of this return to the origin, and then strictly follow like any "funda- mentalist" by definition. On the contrary, this journey to the origins, to the beginning of a genealogy, can best serve to locate the values and structures that have remained common to each democratic and republican tradition, as opposed to the offshoots that have become foreign or even despicable to us, like the "infernal columns" of Turreau.[12] Modern Jacobins admire them still at work in the ranks of the Chetnik militias, with Seselj and Arkan purifying Bosnia of its Muslims, or in colonial or imperial expeditions of all sorts; but these are precisely what I consider the dead branches of the revolutionary republican ideology.

The origins of the French Republic lie in England. The French did not invent everything: the English were the first to decapitate a king and proclaim a Republic. They were the first, while restoring the monarchy, to start the movement towards representative democracy.

If I consider Hobbes to be an exceptional author, it is perhaps because he was in fact the first and most profound modern *Franco-British* political thinker. And maybe the last.

Hobbes is one of the rare early Enlightenment thinkers who wanted to include civil war, disorder and chaos in his thought. Such a move brings him that much closer to our contemporary concerns. He assimilates the "state of nature" to a war pitting each person against all others, which seems to be the very form of violence that has threatened humanity since the end of the bipolar world destroyed the static, menacing and *protective* architecture of the East-West Cold War—the double, global Leviathan. Hobbes, moreover, is not a Cartesian and in France he could be useful to put a check on the logical rationalism that sometimes prevents us from grasping the reemergence of dark, primordial social objects. When Descartes said, "I think therefore I am," Hobbes, who hated metaphysics, replied, "I think therefore matter thinks," thoroughly enchanting Diderot, his biographer in the *Hobbism* article of the *Grande Encyclopédie*. Hobbes is insolent, or rather *ironic*, like Socrates. The polar opposite of a doctor of law. Contrary to Socrates, however, he is extremely dogmatic in appearance and thinks he understood everything and explained it all, but not all phenomena; he understood and explained above all his own method.

He wanted to examine the notion of power, exclusively from an analytical and theoretical standpoint. "I speak not of Man, but, abstractly, of the seat of power," he wrote.[13] For Hobbes, Plato was a dreamer and medieval scholars were absurd dogmatists who wanted to combine Aristotle and the Scriptures. He considered himself ready to "turn away from fantastic obscurity." He claimed, after others, that *homo homini lupus* in order to base his theory of power on something other than the idea that humans have been an angels to each other since the Incarnation of Christ. To forge peace from war, man must reason at least as much as, and even more than, those who forge war from peace.

Through his empirical observations and his constant topic, the chronicle of the disorder and crisis of the Revolution and the English Commonwealth, Hobbes is an *anthropologist of irrevocable decisions in the sphere of danger*. He is in this sense a *strategist* in the same way that Sun Tzu, Tacitus and Clausewitz can be seen as members of this "profession." His statements remain relevant to the questions formulated today by our strategic perplexity when confronted with the horrors of violent social decomposition that fill the news.

Hobbes believed he had introduced the material stability and rigor of the physical or biological sciences into the study of power, while in fact he merely profited from the *crisis* of the English monarchy as an experience of chaos. He claimed[14] to offer a theoretical analysis of the state, entirely furnished by the history of the cycle, apparently self-contained, of the English Revolution. Through an abusive use of his own doctrine, he assimilated it to the decomposition of an artificial mechanism into its natural parts. His first steps towards the Enlightenment can be found in this method, whose inspiration he received from Galileo and Gassendi, providing his thoughts with the mechanistic rigor of the period. This approach obliged him to "dismantle the clockwork," considering the machine of the state as an artifact, an "artificial man." Or rather, this machine made of men. With the English Civil War and the history of the Commonwealth, Hobbes had the advantage of witnessing a life-sized dismantling experiment.

When searching for the rights of the state and the obligations of its citizens, he wrote, one must act "as if the Commonwealth were dissolved," in other words consider what is most natural in men, what makes them capable or incapable of forming governments, and "how those who wish to gather and form a Commonwealth should be disposed." Like a naturalist, Hobbes examined the parts and the whole with the same concern for nomenclature as an entomologist or a mechanic. Each piece or morsel of the dismembered state was given a name and a function. Nothing, not even the king, escaped the cruel bite of his scalpel and functionalist classifications.

However, the object of his research, the state, turns out not to be a whole, as his method would have it, nor is it a finished project like a clock. It is an evolving machine, constantly dismantled in part and partially perfected by human *art*, imagination and liberty. A makeshift machine in constant evolution.

The mechanistic method he preaches is therefore not exactly the one he practiced in his analysis of the English crisis. His explanatory conclusions were all the more precarious in that he put *the chaos of nature*, the raw material of political order, at the heart not only of his subject (power) but of his method: *the analysis of construction through the destruction of power*.

In practice, Hobbes proposes a dialectical analysis of conflict. In theory he is not far from a much more complex historical materialism than the mechanistic materialism of Gassendi. Expressed in terms of a regression to the state of nature, some of his approaches are innovative choices of properly strategic decisions. This is what he said in *de Cive*, in 1642, concerning the regression to war which pits each person against everyone else in the disorder of a civil war: "In the mutual fear that each man feels, everyone has the freedom to use his natural faculties in order to preserve his life and limbs as much as possible." This *freedom*, this right with no theological foundation, is a *natural power* of humankind.

In strategic terms, it would translate as follows: in situations of crisis (for self-defense), human freedom to use these "natural faculties" (instead of the "artificial faculties" proposed by the state) is a human *strategic capacity*. Not as a "natural individual," but as a responsible person from the start, a *potential citizen* is capable of providing an "artificial" power of defense and collective protection. In times of crisis each person has a can-will-should-know-how that must be defined not only as the faculty to choose the most "micro" level of organizing the Sovereign—the family or even the individual—but not the state. This regression to the individual level is a special case, but it is within human capacity *in general* to choose a different, new scale for organizing the Sovereign; to choose a *new level* of sovereignty; and moreover to support a *new type* of sovereignty (monarchy or oligarchy or republic).

Freedom is a human strategic capacity. It can lead to chaos, to a revolution or to political reform.

Foucault, Reader of Hobbes

At this point in our reading of Hobbes, it is worthwhile to introduce the reading Michel Foucault offered more than twenty years ago, in other words before the massive neoliberal, anti-democratic offensive that we are now experiencing.

Hobbes is such a central figure in Foucault's process of reflection on war and violence that he claims to do "exactly the opposite of what Hobbes wanted to do in *Leviathan*."[15]

Foucault gave an imprecise definition of Hobbes in 1976 that he uses as a counter-example. While his own method no doubt benefited from this approach, Hobbes himself was rather man-handled and misread.

Foucault thought he was proceeding in the opposite direction when he stated: "Rather than raising the problem of the central soul (of the Sovereign), try to study instead the multiple, peripheral bodies, bodies established as subjects, through the effect of powers." By rejecting the idea of having to consider this object, the state or the Sovereign, as the direct organizational principle of the individuals, Foucault favored a sort of basic atomism. Yet immediately after, he stated that at least "the individual does not form a sort of primitive atom." The individual is an *effect of power*. But of what power? Of "regional powers that are exercised through infinitesimal techniques and tactics."

Foucault refused to start from the top and always preferred "starting from the bottom." Yet, at the same time, he refused to start from the bottommost point, the individual, a political construct born much later in the liberal individualism of the 18th century; he started from micro-sociological structures that create the basic collective disciplines, and thus *power*: "families," "the medical profession," "public notables," etc. In the end, global domination, the centralized power of the state, was not *pluralized, but on the contrary, pluralized regional domination is globalized.*[16]

I am not seeking to reconcile Foucault and Hobbes, but I think it is in the interest of establishing the genealogy of Sovereignty as we need it today that we should clarify the fruitful misunderstandings present in this transhistoric debate in 1976. We will realize that the inversion of Hobbes Foucault claimed to perform is in fact highly Hobbesian.

Foucault criticized Hobbes' *construction* of Leviathan; however, the key to the construction of Leviathan, as we have seen, is to be found in the *deconstruction* of Behemoth, in other words in the problem Hobbes sought to deal with in his reflections on the English Civil War—what happens to sovereignty when the Sovereign disappears?

Returning to the notion of "regional power" in Foucault, it would be necessary to say that every civil war, or each serious political disturbance, is made up of strategic choices by local or individual regional powers aimed at the survival of these powers in the absence of protection from a higher level (it has been destroyed). As for the individual, he or she is the result of a secession at the smallest level, naturally "atomic" and biologically (though not strategically) indivisible. The individual level is not a "state of nature" for humankind. If the individual under threat is no longer a sovereign level in the organization of protection, the secession of madness (schizophrenia), or the delirious reorganization of the outside world (paranoia), or political suicide, can still intervene as the final protest of strategic sovereignty, the protest of the basic interior collective. The individual is a sovereign authority culturally, in other words strategically, but not naturally, or biologically.

This does not tell us what kinds of strategies and powers are involved at each scale. But in a revolutionary process, strategies are deployed everywhere, at every level, and provide lines of flight or lines of new resistance for the imagination. Each civil war can be at once or contradictorily a war of *class secession* and a war of *community secession*. There are class secessions, but also secessions of provincial sovereignty, of individual survival strategies. In the space-time of the death threat, some types of provisional legitimacy are established with amazing speed and whatever their name may be, in every disturbance they quickly become tools for communicating the situation, the people involved, the stakes, the threats to security. Sometimes they disappear, other times they become historically sovereign identities: the *Cobras* captured Brazzaville in 1997 along with its petroleum. Who will remember the Cobras?

Leviathan and Behemoth

Behemoth is the story of the cycle of the English Civil War and Commonwealth considered as a revolution, in other words (it was understood at the time and still is today in the astronomical sense) as the movement of a planet returning to its point of departure after a complete voyage around the sun. It describes a crisis that topples royal power only to reinstate it in the end. The crisis itself is considered to be a deconstruction of sovereignty into its elements. This crisis must be seen as a theoretical experiment provided by history to give an answer to the question of the essence of sovereignty.

Hobbes is convinced that the best form for the Sovereign is embodied in absolute monarchy, a preference that can already be found in the work of Bodin, who was the first to describe the Sovereign in the *Six Books of the Republic* (1576). Absolute monarchy already was an established French progressive myth at the time. Richelieu was trying to concretize it with Louis XIII in order to bring to an end all the powers based on the medieval orders. Charles I tried to imitate this absolutism when he ceased convening Parliament, an act that was immediately interpreted as tyrannical.

While remaining an absolutist, Hobbes nevertheless remained attached to the Christian idea that *power* came "from God, and through the people, under God, to the Sovereign," or in this case to the king. From there, power is passed around like a hot potato that cools off the farther away it is from the king (if his power is weak). It would be logical to consider that distancing oneself from the king implies distancing oneself from the people and God. In fact, for Hobbes, even if power originates in the people, the only real trace of this mythical provenance lies in the power of the king. We would say today that the provenance is systemic.

His theoretical conviction is that the more absolute the power of a sovereign, the closer it is to the *functional perfection of the contract between sovereign and people*. This contractual schema could also serve to legitimize the absolute power of the Bolshevist party.

No one has to agree with Hobbes, but it is not false that an absolute sovereign works like a Bolshevist party in as much as it works. This fact does not prevent us from thinking that *acceptance of the functional imperfection of the contract between sovereign and people* is the foundation of true democracy, since the people are in a position to review the contracts they have made with their representatives. It is also clear that the possibility of constant review of these contracts is necessary given perpetual economic and social changes that arise from scientific and technical advances. But such progress did not yet exist at the time. Democracy might have been necessary to correct annual variations in harvests due to climatic changes or the whims of trade, but a monarch independent from oligarchies, concerned for his people and well-informed on both agricultural and commercial questions, could also have played the same role. Scientific and technical progress, along with the constant and unpredictable transformations it causes, make democracy necessary.

It was impossible ideologically and theoretically for Hobbes to say that the House of Commons *represented* the people when he analyzed the rise of parliamentary power in its revolt against Charles I. Not that the concept of representation eluded him, but it did not apply, considering that Parliament was only convened by order of the king, not by the people. Parliament, moreover, was hardly a separate power, but part of a whole made up of the *sitting king and the two houses he convened*.

It then became easy for Hobbes to show that the "Rump

Parliament" that took over the sovereign power after the king's death was merely an *oligarchy*; the power of the Protector Oliver Cromwell only tyranny (in the antique sense of an anti-aristocratic dictator); the power of the officers and armies after Cromwell's death, merely a superior strength, but not a supreme power. General Monk, who finally summoned the king—at the end of the cycle, after the abdication of Richard Cromwell, the heir—merely returned power to the only possible popular and divine sovereignty.

Given that this part of Hobbes' thought thus translated does not seem false or mystifying to us, we can say that his absolute monarchy plays the role of a critical instrument. It does not dismiss democracy as an illusion, but rather the illusory representative institutions that in the form of elected civil or military populism can quietly restructure sovereignty to benefit the reign of tyrannical oligarchies. What Hobbes denounces is the "Empire's secret," the secret of the Empire, which always betrays the Commonwealth.

Empire, Republic Betrayed

With his archaic monarchism, Hobbes is devilishly critical of everything that destroys popular sovereignty under the veil of constructing it. His description falls short to the extent that he fails to give up the cyclical representation of history that keeps him from picking up the trail of a progress of popular sovereignty through the experience of revolution, even when betrayed.

The shadow of Cromwell hung over the French Revolution. Under the Directorate, on the eve of 18 Brumaire, Fouché compared Bonaparte to Cromwell. "What preoccupied him, I knew then," he wrote in his memoirs, "was the need to combat republican exuberance, to which he could only oppose moderates and bayonets. To me he seemed to be, politically speaking, a lesser Cromwell. He also feared the fate of Ceasar (assassination) without sharing his brilliance or his genius."[17]

General Monk, the restorer of monarchy, is truly a formidable theoretical figure. After Thermidor, he reappeared on the political scene. Napoleon, then still First Consul, was encouraged to restore the monarchy by his brother Lucien. Having succeeded in obtaining the resignation of Carnot, a staunch republican, from the Ministry of War, Lucien was imprudent enough to publish a defense of his monarchical ideas in a tract entitled: *A Parallel between Cromwell, Monk and Bonaparte*. Yet under the influence of Fouché, who had kept acquaintances among the republican Montagnards, Lucien's one fear was to go down in the history of the French Republic as a General Monk (the role of Cromwell, dead, was obviously reserved for Robespierre). Lucien was sent off to an embassy in Spain, and the restoration that took place was not royal, it was an Imperial consecration. For Fouché, still a man of the Old Regime, this coronation was less intended to imitate the restoration of the royalty by Monk than to perform the restoration of the empire of Charlemagne, the Holy Roman Empire, switching from the Germanic nation to the French nation. We know that Pope Pius was not a frightened prelate forced into accepting the whims of a Tyrant when crowning the Emperor on 11 Frimaire of year XIII, but as pope he supported the return to the Roman Empire. Fouché took part in the coronation, but his presence, immortalized by David better than any live television broadcast, was only justified by the wizened condition of the Holy Father and the self-coronation of Napoleon. For Fouché, whose expression in the painting lacks enthusiasm, the coronation was no doubt a simoniac *unction* that would have horrified Hobbes, as we will see.

The English Parliament members, regicide revolutionaries,

were archaic, for they were religious, but as divided, impassioned and radical as those that followed them in France 150 years later; they had determined very precisely the places where constitutional innovation had to break through the medieval theory of sovereignty.

Perhaps not by theoretical deduction, but as strategists, because they were obliged to make decisions in the face of danger. By means of votes and laws they attempted to remove the points that called their *power* into question, points that Hobbes carefully identified, starting with the point connecting the king's head to his chest that was removed in 1649. They decided that the Parliament could convene automatically each year *by the calendar* without being summoned by the king, and that it could meet without the king. They decided that the House of Lords only represented the lords and that the people, fully represented by the Commons, could pass laws without the Lords. Over the course of the 18th, 19th and 20th centuries, these reforms were also imposed on the English monarchy by the Lords; they had been present since the first half of the 17th century, and seemed to demonstrate with slow continuity a logic contrary to that of the absolutism of Hobbes. The evolution has continued to this day, with the final crisis of the British monarchy and its transformation, with Lady Diana, into a media-saturated humanitarian institution on par with the Monaco royalty, an operation that was well worth a second capital execution.

One might think that Hobbes has been beaten by history, that his approach is "reactionary" and his theory incapable of describing the relationship between the real forces of English society and the future of European democracy. Nonetheless, Diderot praised him in the *Hobbism* article of the Encyclopédie published in 1765 in Neuchâtel, 77 years after the Glorious Revolution of 1688, but

10 years before the American Revolution and 26 years before the French Revolution. Hobbes, on the contrary, considered himself a founder of critical political science. He opened holes in his own absolutist theory and shed more light than others on the question of the ambiguous use of violence as a fundamental and / or destructive part of the state and of sovereignty.

Two key moments of his life and approach give a more relative idea of his monarchical ideology. I only mention them here in respect to a perspective that is equally viable for contemporary disturbances.

Exile as Protection
First there was the episode of his flight from Paris and return to England in 1651, after the publication of *Leviathan* under the English Republic of Cromwell.

Intellectually, Hobbes was a brave coward. He would rather run away than change a single word of his texts. He had escaped England once before in 1640, already the theoretician of absolutism but hostile to *divine right* royalty, when he felt that the monarchy was threatened by religious uprisings and by Presbyterian and Puritan fanaticism. He fled to France without awaiting the execution of the king.

As history would have it, in 1651, after 11 years in France, in the middle of the uprising of the nobility known as the Fronde, Hobbes was frightened by allegations that had begun to circulate against him in the court of Louis XIII among the exiled English monarchists accompanying Charles II, the dethroned Prince of Wales for whom Hobbes had served as tutor. These hostile accusations were based on his theory of *protection*: "*The obligation of subjects to the Sovereign is understood to last as long, and no longer, than the power lasteth by which he is able to protect them.*" [18]

This phrase, according to Diderot, aroused suspicion concerning the allegiance of Hobbes to his king "who was reduced to such an extreme state that his subjects could await no help from him." The young king of France, the regent Anne d'Autriche and the minister Mazarin were themselves in an unstable position. *Leviathan* reads: "When in a war, foreign or domestic, the enemies get a final victory, and the forces of the Commonwealth no longer keeping the field the subjects cannot expect any more protection in return for their loyalty, then is the Commonwealth dissolved, and every man is at liberty to protect himself by such courses as his own discretion shall suggest unto him."[19]

The incriminating passage takes up the theme that I have called the "secession of strategic levels," and is more theoretical than against the monarchy.

In contemporary terms, we would say that the contract of protection between the people and the sovereign-king is established for an indefinite period of time, but that it becomes void if the person in charge is fired. If the Sovereign fails to provide adequate protection, it amounts to a breach of contract. Since the protective function is based on violence, losing control of that force, losing his monopoly or evident superiority, would imply the loss of his role as Protector and thus to his end as Sovereign. At that point, everyone (unfortunately, according to Hobbes) regains his or her natural right to self-protection and society falls back into the "state of nature," unless a new sovereign protector appears.

This seems to open the door to all types of opportunism and collaborationism until one looks more closely at the sentence that clearly states that the enemy must have *won a final victory* and that *the forces of the Sovereign can no longer continue to fight*. In

Hobbesian terms, Gaullism had the particular quality of insisting that the war in France was not over and that a handful of Free French, the forces of the French Republic, continued to fight.

Citizens must decide for themselves, or in their sovereign debates, whether or not the battle is over and whether the forces of the Republic continue to fight. Hobbes could tell that the exiled nobles flocking to the court of a dispossessed king who held a claim to the English throne, lacked the strength of citizens and were no longer fighting.

As it stands, this brief passage from *Leviathan*, which is at the heart of the approach found in *Behemoth* (written and published much later), is probably the center piece of the *perplexity* of Hobbes. It is so central that he felt truly threatened and took flight from the courts of Louis XIII and Charles II rather than facing the intrigues that insinuated he was in favor of Cromwell. He was not the type to take back what he had said and, in fact, if we continue to use strategic vocabulary and consider the Sovereign to be a decision maker, he truly did seem to put the Sovereign in a position of *responsibility* in the realm of danger: only his own errors would cause him to stop being the Sovereign.

But is it a question of strategy, of a rational decision in the sphere of danger? *Theoretically*, it is not: the responsibility of the Sovereign is that of an automaton. Hobbes was a royalist, and close to his former student the Prince of Wales, but even if he believed that the Prince's claim to the throne after his father's execution was legitimate, etc., for Hobbes the Sovereign, the Commonwealth, the Republic, the state are still not a proprietary monarchy to which loyalty is due by inheritance, but instead an "artificial animal" or even an "artificial man" created by natural man. Hobbes stated this opinion in the opening pages of *Leviathan*. The Sovereign is no more *responsible* for his protective function than a computer is responsible for its memory and programs. The short sentence with which his royalist enemies found fault was for Hobbes a sort of atemporal tautology. The mechanistic theories he inherited from Gassendi prevented him from thinking otherwise. The clock can be dismantled and rebuilt in order to understand how it works, but this does not change the way it works.

Sovereign is he who protects the people by force from the war pitting each person against everyone else. "Is not sovereign he who cannot"—or can no longer—protect by force the people from the war of each person against every other... For the mechanistic Hobbes, these propositions were strictly equivalent. If he had said for example that "the king remains Sovereign even if he is incapable of protecting the people from the war of every man against every man," he would have undermined his entire approach.

We could add the following to the list of tautologies: "Is not yet Sovereign he who cannot yet protect the people by force from the war pitting each person against everyone else." But as soon as the people can protect themselves, they become sovereign:

> Tremblez ennemis de la France:
> Rois ivres de sang et d'orgueil,
> Le peuple souverain s'avance,
> Tyrans descendez au cercueil.[20]

The Song of Departure, dear to the French's republican ancestors, is perfectly explicit: the sovereign people brings monarchies (presumed to be aristocratic powers) as well as tyrannies (which are popular powers) to their knees. The subtle distinction between kings and tyrants disappears if the People are completely sovereign. Here, the monarchism of Hobbes is reduced to an archaic affect, but his theory remains resilient.

Causes of War

A key point in the theoretical perplexity of Hobbes is the definition of the precise moment when government power is totally destroyed during a civil war. The reference here is to *Behemoth*, a work that was written after the restoration of the monarchy in England at the time Hobbes had nothing left to fear. The king, his protector, forgave him his escape from France, but never authorized an official publication in England of the work with the all too controversial subject matter. The new work, however, contrary to his flight and exile, was a theoretical work rather than a "practical" conceptualization. What is the best moment to destroy the Sovereign and for what reasons? For Hobbes, in *Behemoth*, the power of the Sovereign self-destructs under the regime of a Commonwealth. With the late publication of this book in 1668, well after the restoration of the monarchy, Hobbes had the leisure to theorize freely, without fear of falling prey to courtly intrigues. He did not, however, recognize the phase of self-destruction unreservedly as the execution of the king in 1649, even if the king's beheading can be attributed to decidedly suicidal behavior (a model that Louis XVI apparently chose not to follow by fleeing to Varennes). The struggle of every person against everyone else appears prior to the death of the monarch in the form of the quarrels between politico-religious factions and it was followed by the parliamentary disorder that bore a strong resemblance to general war.

For Hobbes, parliamentary conflict was not the cause of the destruction of the Sovereign; *religious* conflict was. Himself a believer, Hobbes despised all religious influence in political matters for a theological reason that he clearly established, but one that we can consider a *strategic* reason given his treatment of the subject.

The papal ambition to dominate the Roman Empire as well as the Emperor's ambition to control the clergy and the Pope, each had been part of the history of Christianity since Constantine the Great. Christian anti-clericalism exists and is much more virulent than the weakened form prevalent in the secular nation-state. What we sometimes forget is that this criticism, fundamental for the temporal power of the clergy, is directly related to questions of war and peace, to the defense of the *republic of peace*, to Christianity, in other words to peace in Europe. The criticism does not bear on the *temporal* power of the clergy, but on the use of its *spiritual* power to send people into military conflict, a completely different story that can be considered to be *simony*.

Selling the sacraments and indulgence is only one aspect of simony. Another would be to lead men to war through a realignment of the doctrine of Christ meant to organize predatory force, a salaried offensive army.

The most established form of simony, selling sacraments, comes from the ordinary corruption of the Church by the sympathetic and peaceful values of commerce, which make it such a financial power. A second logic lies behind this prohibition: it also seeks to maintain the uniquely pacific qualities of Christianity and its hostility towards any incidence of hatred and violence. This is part of the fundamental program of Christianity, just as it is for Buddhism. The Church is not supposed to accumulate riches by commercializing its sacraments, because if it did, it would become a worldly power capable of stockpiling wealth, defending its treasury, hiring mercenaries to protect it, making money by using these warriors to exploit others, in short, of living and dying by the sword, like a nation.

This capability is reserved for the king or the emperor, and this strategic prohibition concerns both the accumulation of wealth (coins bearing the likeness of the Sovereign must return to Caesar through taxation) and the use of war (Caesar raises taxes to launch a campaign). Holding back taxes, withholding from Caesar the objects that bear his image, is an act of war. This was not contrary to a certain Jewish vision of the realm of the Messiah, but was condemned by Christianity.

Finally, there is a still more perverse way to establish a rich, violent and political church through the direct use of the discourse of salvation: the church should not directly exercise its pastoral and mystical capabilities to induce the faithful to sacrifice (even freely) their life for the clergy. The origins of the modern conflicts that developed in the 16th and 17th centuries during the Reform (followed by the desire of the Absolute Monarchy to submit the clergy to its control) can be found in the medieval conflict between the pope and the emperor. The central position of the Catholic Church in questions of war and peace between Christians or Christian kingdoms as well as with the rest of the world, was a question that was debated throughout the Middle Ages. The "temporal" and "spiritual" powers accused each other of provoking (unjust) wars between Christians and each claimed the sole right to enforce the peace that both God and human reason desired. The righteousness of a crusade was more problematic for Christianity than a jihad for Islam.

The apparently extreme modernity of Hobbes comes from the process of emergence of the anti-clerical medieval state. In 1324, in his *Defensor Pacis*, Marsilius of Padua sought to shake the foundations of the Vatican's claim for pre-eminence. He argued that, from the beginning, control of the (Germanic) Holy Roman Empire was passed down *by election* (election by the princes, some of whom were German prince-bishops) and not at all by papal decree. The Pope in Rome could only confirm the vote and,

Marsilius wrote, "he does not make the emperor any more than the Bishop of Reims makes the King of France." Using a method similar to the one Hobbes would later choose, Marsilius decided that the origin of sovereign power can be more clearly verified in its mechanisms, by its means of renewal and real transmission, than in any legend surrounding its foundation.

By the 14th century, religious authority and political power were separated by method, though this separation was obviously for theological purposes specific to Christianity. It was also, more concretely, a predatory and financial question. How much money can be taken from the faithful out of fear of war, religious respect, or protection by arms? How much from the threat of excommunication, fear of damnation and the right of absolving sins held by the clergy? Violence and security on the one hand, threat of damnation and promise of heaven on the other, are the two principal means of acquiring wealth during the Middle Ages. For Marsilius of Padua, *this predatory duality is the cause of war within the Christian world*. The duality of financial power necessarily leads to a bipolar military situation. In Italy, the Guelfes and Gibelins were the opposing parties. The Pope exceeded his rightful domain when he attempted to dominate the emperor by religious means and to dominate the Christian world with the Crusades, or the "fires of excommunication."

Marsilius of Padua had already defined peace, order and unity within the state in terms of coercion, and it is by the monopoly of control over this coercion that the function of the *unique sovereign* (who can be an oligarchy, a civil assembly or a monarch) is a sufficient condition for peace.[21] The cause of civil war lies in the papacy's ambition to establish the clergy as a legitimate force against the more properly political power. Marsilius struck out against "the false opinion of certain bishops of Rome and their perverted desire to

importance, rights that are held by those who hold sovereignty over the Commonwealth. Whence the fundamental principle of the Hobbesian critique of the clergy:

"It is impossible a Commonwealth should stand where any other than the Sovereign hath a power of giving greater rewards than life and of inflicting greater punishments than death."[26]

By promising eternal life or eternal death, the ambitions of superiority that a global religious power entertains over a politico-military power cause the destruction of sovereign institutions and the disappearance of all protection. They provoke the war of everyone against everyone else. For Hobbes, the Sovereign did not disappear because of Cromwell, but because of the religious motivations of the opposing armies.

Three Camps against Three Powers and the End of Sovereign

It remains to be seen *when* exactly sovereignty disappeared during the course of the English Revolution. Perhaps it was at the time when many different clergies—at least three: the Catholics, Presbyterians and Puritans as popular clergies—claimed the right to make proclamations in competition with the king, the right to define rewards greater than life and punishments worse than death. Out of all the different religious groups, only the Anglicans declared themselves *not to be in competition with the king*, while rejecting the simoniac power of the Pope.

It is only half true that Hobbes recognized the legitimacy of the power of sovereign protection Cromwell attributed himself as Lord Protector. The dictator resolved the religious problem by establishing religious freedom (for all save the papists).

Even if greater disorder ensued from the king's death, the destruction of the Sovereign was not symbolized by the rise of Cromwell to power with the support of the "new army" of his *agitators* elected by the soldiers. The *round heads*, the army of Cromwell, constituted the Sovereign. A global philosophical definition of the destruction of the Sovereign only appeared at the end of the cycle, following the death of Oliver Cromwell, with the split into a *triple power*: the power of the Protector Richard Cromwell, of the Parliament and of the army in early 1659. This marked the end of the protective function.

These three camps were aligned in alliances of two against one. They were thus less a representation of the separation of powers between the executive, legislative and judicial branches (as found in the three powers of Montesquieu and Locke a century later) than a *representation* of the state of nature, of the war of every person against all others. This point merits further consideration. In a state crisis, a three-way war is a simplified version of a war with an infinity of sides, and the *stage of three-way war* can be defined as a recurring paradigm that accompanies the disappearance of the protective function. It has occurred in Lebanon, Bosnia and Colombia; it also appeared in the crisis of 69 AD that almost destroyed the Roman Empire after the death of Nero. The three-way war can be considered the characteristic moment in the destruction of the Sovereign.

Today, the question of whether civil war is a "return to the state of nature" has little meaning. Diderot opposed Hobbes and Rousseau when discussing the well-traveled theme of the good or evil nature of humankind. Yet this inquiry falls short of the fundamental question. A naturally peaceful and "happy," therefore good, humanity is a myth, at least according to what one can observe of the primitive societies still in existence. Some of these societies live in a constant state of war of each one against all others (even if the word war is not necessarily the correct term).[27]

Hobbes thought of human beings "returning to the state of nature" as he was able to observe them at work during the English Civil War, whose disorder allowed concrete self-analyses of the human nature of politics. Humankind appeared neither naturally good nor naturally evil, but "naturally strategic." This might simply mean that control of the limbic system by the frontal lobes is characteristic of our species. But that does not eliminate the limbic system. Contrary to Rousseau, Hobbes built his paradigm on historical experience, but was mistaken in referring to it as a "return to the state of nature"; as Diderot noted, he deduced from his definition of chaos that human nature was evil, and *homo homini lupus*, while man is also a sheep for man as well as a strategic being who mixes these two moments at the level of feelings or pure rationality.

This combination will serve as a basis for value judgements, the definition of war crimes and crimes against humanity, of the combatants as either "good" or "bad."

From Hobbes to Clausewitz

It is always possible to resume Hobbes through his definition of sovereignty as the protection of the people and Clausewitz by his formula that "war is simply the continuation of politics by other means." But in the neo-medieval complexity that we are entering, these definitions do not seem to apply clearly.

These conceptual instruments must be renewed to carry on the democratic fight, to reshape the definition of popular sovereignty as protection and to launch the search for peace again, which is no small matter today, given the return to wars and repression at all levels in the Empire of Disorder, a system that necessarily disrupts the pacific democratic process as the transparent conflicts of class struggles.

According to what remains implicit in Hobbes, we would rather interpret the return to chaos as a strategic choice that all collective or individual "people" must make when faced with just such a situation, when it becomes urgent to recover the use of violence that was the *protective* faculty of the absent sovereign. This faculty had merely been an alienation of violence to ensure the smooth functioning of security and peace through the artificial person of the Sovereign.

To put it briefly: a crisis within the state should not be confused with a return to the state of nature. It would be more appropriate to say that the foundations of the state reappear at the microsociological level.

We might choose to remain perplexed at this point, however, for, since the 18th century, we have been used to mentioning social classes as one of the possible divisions of social reality. There are no social classes in Hobbes. Moreover, in our modern crises between communities, class distinctions often disappear, or their secessionist logic is repressed as illegitimate or unconscious: the right of the Plebe to return to the Aventine Hill in Rome seems unthinkable. Only communities have the right to secede. Class consciousness and class struggle vanish in this way, even during civil wars. A number of civil wars showed class consciousness or class struggle playing a full role in internal conflicts to such an extent that since 1848, or at least since the Paris Commune, it has become our habit to think that the struggle between rich and poor classes lies at the heart of all contemporary civil wars and that suspending this struggle is the essence of democracy. Classes as well as communities are fighting to change the hierarchy. But struggles between communities and their adjournment have nothing to do with democracy defined as a suspension of class warfare. They can even prevent its foundations from being laid. How should we change this model?

3. Hobbes-Clausewitz

Looking at the world today before any theoretical intervention, just as a lyrical spectacle, I can observe at least one hierarchy. I see the kingdoms and republics of the world threatened by soft Balkanization, toppled to the ground, groveling at the feet of the American Empire of Disorder that encompasses them. The little kings, the heroic or craven nobility, all the peoples of the world can all watch them via the wonders of television. The terrible massacres fill the minds of the world with a growing sense of powerlessness. Not that there are more massacres than before, but now each one is common knowledge, displayed like a warning for all peoples, or pandered as an imperial drug like the circus games in Rome condemned by the Fathers of the Church at the end of the Empire. Torture, rape, mutilation and mangled corpses have become common sights thanks to the exploits of Mr. Tudjman, Boban, Karadzic, Milosevic in ex-Yugoslavia, or the troops of Mr. Putin in ex-USSR, new tsars who have risen to power through pogroms. Mr. Tudjman was lucky enough to die before standing trial. But pogroms can take place without tsars: the Hutu militias in Rwanda, the paramilitaries in Colombia, the military or religious assassins in Algeria. The softer approach of apartheid, humiliation and the slow destruction of identity imposed on conquered neighbors reduced to sub-human status, is the method chosen by Netanyahu, Barak or Sharon in Palestine, and by the Turkish government in Kurdish regions. In many areas, military, civil or religious tyranny has made a comeback founded on aborting democracy, economic failure and barbaric violence. Power relationships having become increasingly asymmetrical since the 1960s and 70s, and the strategic standpoint of resistance reduced to powerlessness, the younger generations have turned to terrorism, hostage taking and counter-cruelty. At the same time, as if by blind denial, the triumph of universal human rights has been declared, rights that are violated everywhere disorder reigns. For neither their *protection* or their *violation* are regulated by the center of the Empire of Disorder, which prevents the UN from intervening and refuses to sign binding international conventions, rather by commandos of masked military, or para-military, assassins working for uprooted financial interests, and sometimes by global uprooted mafias, a new phenomenon.

Confronted today with this global fascism and its small local servants, intellectuals can no longer content themselves with reasserting the supremacy of intelligence and reason in the face of the material brutality of the Beast. They must really put their intelligence at the disposal of those forces that are capable of directly confronting this evil of the global dynamics leading the 21st century towards the generalization of horror.

Those who want no part in the confrontation will not read the "bad news." If they fall into the social rubbish heap (like the middle class in Argentina, the only one to be hit full on at this time), they can accuse themselves of stupidity or strategic mistakes. The others have to take stock of the ways to resist this widespread insanity, even more serious in its extent than the Nazi madness that rocked my childhood like a recurrent nightmare. I think that fascism can be easily defined in Hobbesian terms by the fact that *children are afraid* because the *adults are afraid*. There is no longer any *protection* worth the name, only the hierarchy of violence remains. Fixing hierarchies is the only way of stabilizing a political formation. But is it possible in the Empire of Disorder?

Lenin was often wrong, both during his life and after his death. The supreme—hence final—phase of capitalism is not imperialism. Unless imperialism is finally, *essentially*, not the export of capital to colonial zones, but its constant relocation in free market globalization. The strength of multinational conglomerates and delocalized banks, the transformation of investments into temporary installations as volatile as off-shore accounts that hold the threat of relocation over their workers, create a structural fear. The uprooting of the threat produces a structural fear by rendering localized protection useless.

The threat of unemployment is enough to cause fear. But to *terrify*, massacres or hyperinflation are needed. Globalization today is not supreme because it has not yet organized a *politico-military* system *in conformity with the financial system*, the way Lenin proposed "imperialism" as a concept for the spatial organization of the relocation of capital into the colonial or neo-colonial empires of vast industrial nations. Today, there is no global Empire that proposes a global political regime. There is no violence in conformity with the economy. We can imagine even further stages of development, other wars more global than nuclear war—which never occurred—or than the wars in Chechnya and Kosovo; and other types of peace even closer to the "peace of cemeteries." But we can also imagine a peace more heavenly than the Dayton Agreement.

In the meantime, before saying politics is dead, we need to point out and zoom in on each place where *creative sovereignty* appears, locating where new forms of politics are taking shape in the world and finding where politics is hiding on both sides. Finding out which elites have organized oligarchic politics into a sovereign force without the people, and in which new or old groups popular sovereignty has taken hold and is coordinated outside the ordinary framework of democracy.

The culture of electoral democracy has particularly weakened the notion of politics. The idea that politics must necessarily take the form of a transparent, electoral and parliamentary democracy with eligible parties on the left and on the right, with a normal level of corruption instead of massacres, has perverted our sense of the stakes involved. One need not adhere to conspiracy theories in order to admit that oligarchic, and therefore antidemocratic, sovereignties and empires exist. Working to clearly define these phenomena is necessary for an effective reorganization of the left. The American program of "democracy for all" is all well and good, but it sounds like a missionary toasting at a cannibal banquet. The problem must be dealt with at its source. There can be no democracy without the victory of popular power over the oligarchy.

Corporate Sovereignty and State Interests

In the world today, there is a serious disturbance in the representation of *political* identity and thus of sovereignty. In order to avoid being nothing or nobody, to avoid a loss of sovereignty, people rely on their god, their language, their tribe, their town or their family.

Yet the greatest disturbance is not caused by this mere return to the interwoven sovereignties of the middle ages that leads to a hesitation between the legitimacy of ethno-historical *laender*, of nation-states and the legitimacy of Europe or the universal Atlantic empire. This greatest disturbance results from the opposition between political sovereignty of varying degrees and the private sovereignty of private corporations (they are not usually considered sovereignties but rather "private interests"). This conception belongs to the past since the hierarchy of power has been reversed. If only to express our indignation or concern for this change, we are now obliged to say that corporate sovereignty comes first, and the interests of the state last.

It has long been held that the essential power of capital is found in the corporation, be it involved in production, commercialization or credit. However, it is naive to believe that corporate leaders are merely a functional group that reproduces itself, by following the scientific laws of economics and respecting "good governance." This idea is restrictive because it overlooks its political implications. It merely repeats the most common postulates of popularized Marxism by placing the "economy" at the helm of human evolution. Corporate leaders of today are involved in politics. Even if the economy remains *determinant*, politics *decides*.

Who started Globalization? Corporations that put a considerable emphasis on internationalization and moved from an international to a global economy, and from multinational strategies to global ones, shifting from a political strategy of "respecting national sovereignty" to a "logic of transnational networks."[28] The problems involving corporate identity are dealt with by merger decisions and the search for new identities. In short, they are political problems.

Corporations, or rather their leaders, have reached forms of sovereignty that are foreign to the territorial definition of states. This is not a conspiracy, just the state of the world. On the one hand, this situation derives from the transnationalization of violent mafias; on the other, from the transnationalization and concentration of capital, especially financial capital. Colombian, Afghan, Pakistani, Nigerian drug mafias, Russian and Yugoslavian mafias, Chinese Triads, the Camorra, the N'dranghetta, etc., all make up a world of private, violent and popular enterprises with wealth and power. They harbor certain symbols of sovereignty such as "the legitimate use of the threat of death." Mafia legitimacy is a political construction that is *at war* with certain states, but sometimes allied with powerful states (Mexico, Russia) or tiny ones (Liechtenstein). Although they do not comprise or dominate the majority of entrepreneurial society, they contribute to the destabilization of the government and the breakdown of the protective function that is legitimately ensured by the nation-state. They are a new global neighbor for corporations.

But the relationship of war or alliance with states also characterizes industrial corporations, distinct from the Mafia, which have increasingly become conglomerates that contest any form of regulation. Regulations once allowed nations to manage a certain distribution of resources between rich and poor. The wars or alliances with different nations are sought in the name of free trade. Over the past few years, private corporations have substantially regrouped and concentrated their efforts and now these new conglomerates exercise their considerable weight on governments. Their directors are considered the equals of the President of the United States, and often wield more power than the heads of state of smaller countries.

Freely organized crime, freely organized finance and freely organized industrial or commercial corporations have become allies to defend free trade, and it is extremely difficult to locate the real, that is to say the financial boundary between the criminal economy and the transnational economy in general.

Cruel Little Wars

To defend themselves as corporations, the governments of developing nations only have two options at their disposal:
- either to act like mere "provincial governors" in the global empire of Capital, applying the recommendations of the IMF (or abandoning them if they are out of style);
- or to act as independent warlords to gain a foothold elsewhere than in the pure economic space where mega-corporations and macro-banks already have the upper hand.

Lacking support from the start, as warriors, from the real power of transnational capital, government structures can only hope to wage independently two limited types of war (which may be combined):
- an offensive war aimed at occupying and controlling neighboring countries, a sort of paleo-micro-colonialism within a region. (This is the case for many current wars in Africa, Israel, and for Turkey in Cyprus.);
- or a war of Balkanization, an internal conflict transformed into an external war, leading to a reduction to the scale of identities, or to maintaining internal, archaic, imperial mini-structures by means of genocide and *internal* oppression of the proscribed group. (Apartheid on the level of the district or of the town.)

For a perfect example of the combination of these two types of war one need only consider the case of Serbia.

These violent mini-systems can create regional wars and destruction, but they require allies to provide them with ressources and they are forced to turn to the only branch of international capital that deals in both finance and violence, the Mafia networks. One could say that these small, genocidal local wars are supported by a Mafia economy (mostly Russian nowadays), but one could also say that the Mafia economy uses these savage little wars to reinforce and protect its own share of the global financial market. These cruel little wars are in a some way the exterior Clausewitzian wars of the stateless and landless Mafia system, a continuation of politics through other means. For the Mafias they are a continuation of politics through other means, violent means. The physical flow of Mafia arms and funds allows us to identify one enemy as a branch of the corporations that control international capital.

It is not enough to think we have succeeded in dividing the world into the Good Guys and Bad Guys. Distinguishing between Mafia and non-Mafia economy is somewhat misleading. The preceding analysis remains inadequate, precisely because "dirty" money and the "normal" flow of global finance communicate directly and thus there is no (non-geographical) equivalent of a "natural" frontier between the two financial entities. Money has no odor and any amount invested loses its identity; unlike oil and vinegar, different deposits do not remain separated. We can distinguish between different lines in an accountant's ledger, if it is not secret, but if we're investigating to uncover banking secrets, we are wasting our time. Even if final "punishments" exist, there is no systematic control. The financial effects and global consequences are immediate. The system is not really divided into antagonistic and autonomous subsystems: choosing between

Mafia money and non-Mafia money, using one against the other, is the only way to establish a boundary; only human beings can be clean or dirty. The fight for peace must therefore either master the connection between the two and *establish this frontier* by any means necessary at the level of *corporate politics*, of its continuation of politics through war.

The boundary is between human beings, and not capital. If it is not politically established as soon as possible, peace and even the very notion of peace will be lost for generations to come. This is how war becomes a continuation of politics and this connection must be recognized as part of the new spatio-temporal organization of global relocation.

What does it mean to bet on the existence of—and create alliances with—non-Mafia capital management? It can only be concretely defined in terms of the well-defined geopolitical spaces of *habitats*: cities, countries, regions, continents. It would imply a modification in some circulation of capital by obliging its owners to put their feet back on the ground, to make concessions concerning delocalization and asocial definitions of investment. This is the abstract idea behind the Tobin Tax: slow the movement of capital by taxing the instability of investment havens. Government "intervention" at the politico-military level of confrontations is not unthinkable; it is aimed at the decision makers and money handlers who do not concretely invest in the economy, only in their own speculations; it is not a decision against "dirty" money. Dirty money cannot be attacked directly, so this would be an intervention against one of the more negative aspects of global financial capital, its precariousness. Dirty money would not necessarily be the most affected by the Tobin Tax. Mafia money is often reinvested in goods, funds and national companies, because it is obtained through death threats and at the risk of life and limb.

As a consequence, elite Mafia members have long been more affective and archaic, expressing a form of local patriotism. They build palaces in their hometown, buying thousands of acres to take on the airs of new local nobility. This attitude is on its way out, however, with the arrival of the Russian Mafia and computerized tax havens. Yet the use of violence remains the realm of the different Mafias, as well as the attraction of making quick profits through arms trafficking and from wars themselves.

Even if they are only private ones, Mafias can be more easily distinguished as political and public enemies, when they act as warlords. And the search for peace stops being the affair of bleating pacifists and starts to become dangerous and courageous. It can even make professional soldiers, who must keep their guns at rest during their UN missions, envy the most heroic NGOs.

The problem merits further development with concrete examples: we have a tendency to consider the upheavals of cruel little wars and their cruel little warriors (Milosevic, Karadjic, Mladic, Tudjman, Seselj and Arkan against the Bosnians and Kosovars in the Balkans; Tutsi and Hutus in Rwanda-Burundi; Israel-Palestine, Lebanon, in the Middle East; paramilitary, military and guerrillas in Latin America; Basques, Irish, Corsicans in the European Union) as archaic leftovers, barbaric but petty combats between little warlords losing their heads over local popularity or inheriting ancient, maladjusted and cynical oligarchies, or heroic, old-regime traditions that have become suicidal. According to the cynical and disabused perspective now common in the new transnational *nomenklatura*, all of the misfits with slow economies and medieval ways, be they from the extreme right or extreme left, religious or secular, Moorish or Christian, have been considered poor adversaries, easily conquered by the triumphant growth of peace-friendly global capital and the inevitable progress of human rights.

First of all, we need to rid ourselves of this Disneyland political logic and face up to the complex system that creates a coherent link between omnipresent violence and the peaceful expansion of the free-market economy. This suicidal system produces both a high concentration of wealth and a general increase of poverty and it can only be regulated by the genocide of the poor. They would reduce the market too significantly for the productive forces unleashed by techno-science.

Secondly, a choice must be made, even in the name of peace, between one violence or another, rather than condemning all violence en masse.

Thirdly, if we wish to contribute to the defeat on the global scale of the force of financial movements that are leading humanity to disaster, we must confront this project, which is already in place, *wherever it induces violence* through interventions meant to neutralize agents of deregulated violence, i.e. paramilitarism and its deadly association with regular armed forces.

It is easy to say "we must do this," "we must do that," but to whom are these prescriptions, in fact *political* recommendations, addressed, when states are starting to weaken?

In Europe, these recommendations can only be aimed at the European Union, not as it is now, but as it should be if it continues its progress towards democracy and the confederation of social republics. It is the only identity that has the form of an alternative global strategic project.

For other continents, it remains to be seen. It certainly depends on the places and on the means of recruitment and organization of the new nobilitary violence that has regained the upper hand over democratic traditions and the political expertise of popular resistance.

"Nobilitary" Violence

In the history of the Old Regime and in the already plurisecular history of industrial capitalism and the international finance system, the most normal type of "regulation" was violence. State violence or paramilitary violence.

Nobilitary violence and the savage repression of peasant revolts were part of the means of maintaining the inequality of the feudal system. Today, the savage repression of modern revolts of the urban and rural poor benefits the pseudo-nobility of the Global Empire, which can be identified by its "California lifestyle," with private villas, pools and private security in every country of the world, especially in poorer countries where inequality is the most flagrant, but also, of course, in the United States and in Europe. This nobility no longer acts directly, but through the military or paramilitary forces.

There are countries like those in Latin America where the passage was seamless from the nobility of the colonial regimes, made up of *conquistadores* and *encomendieros*, to post-modern oligarchies; where the oppression of the poor has not changed the strategic recipes of the Old Regime, in other words the ones inherited from Antiquity, the Middle Ages, the modernity of the Renaissance and even from the enlightened absolutism of the Bourbons of Spain and the Braganzas of Portugal.

Then, with the rise of industrial and financial capitalism, asymmetric armed violence (the strong versus the weak) became a violent part of the simple accounting principles of profit-seeking enterprises. Asymmetric violence underpinned the colonial conquests and the "unequal treaties" of the 19th and 20th centuries by crushing any uprising that claimed the right to equality as well as to liberty.

Today, the integration of computers into the financial world has led to organizing state violence or paramilitary violence around the elimination of pockets of misery, of "disposable" people massacred at the local level. People become "disposable" when nothing more can be taken from them.

The Places and Times of a New Expansion of War

Political debates are clouded by the opaque mix of political, economic and military sovereignty of different scales and varying levels of openness that are just as interwoven as they are juxtaposed in every local situation. This chaos can seem quite complex, especially if one compares it with the simplified "economy-violence" relationship established within the framework of sovereign nation-states from the 17th to the 19th centuries and subsequently within the East-West polarity.

In some cases, in order to redirect the distribution of wealth by other means than through the hierarchy of financial affairs, regulatory populist movements have appeared with military support that seek to create a redistribution relying on "the rigors of the law" in under-developed countries (Venezuela and Equador with the Chavist phenomenon could be seen as a revival of the Velazquism of the 1970s). These justice-seeking revolts have not necessarily been successful, but the world cannot deny the question they pose.

However, the Clausewitzian garden (in other words, the linking of states) where only military sovereignty can thrive, with its more or less unjust order, has almost lost its power today, and will continue to disappear, even in Europe, which continues to grow by co-opting new nations. Europe is currently the only hub of economic, cultural, politico-military and geographic resistance to unbridled globalization. Japan could also become an important axis. As for China, it has its own particular way of combining a wild free market, central planning and regulation, Communism and Mafia development. For the time being, it cannot follow the European model, but eventually could return to it as the two attempts made in the previous century with Sun Yat Sen and the Communist Party testify. The Americas, the main source of neoliberal thinking, could also in the future become an important part of the struggle against this thought. Mexico, in this regard, forms an odd couple with the United States, and their common future is indispensible, though unpredictable. After the events in Seattle in 1999, the idea that the Americas are the site of an indecipherable contradiction that could eliminate neoliberalism is no longer completely absurd; however, Seattle remains more an example of social awareness than a political turning point. It is therefore imperative for Europe to take a leading role in the *political* formulation of the problem. The relative autonomy of Europe supposes its union but also its new foundation as a democracy. Since the Gulf War, it has developed an increasingly distinguishable identity. It is not in itself an antidote to the dangers that threaten republics, but it serves as the theater for a critical political awareness seeking to control the slide into free market globalism.

Political Continuation: A Genealogy

Clausewitzian "Continuation" or "Perpetuation" (*Fortsetzung*) is a stabilized unit representing the rupture of war / peace (valid for the 18th to the 20th centuries). It has developed progressively over the course of history though less in the philosophical consciousness of Clausewitz (Raymond Aron tried to prove it in his *Clausewitz*) than in the genealogy of the war / peace boundary and the notion of the state connected to the idea of progress.

A brief exercise in critical attention will reveal how Clausewitzian *continuation* is an avatar (a reincarnation, a fixture) of Hobbesian sovereignty established on an implicit contract between the people, who reject the state of war, and the Sovereign, an artificial object responsible for managing this contract like a program designed from the bottom up.

Clausewitz wrote: *War is simply (*bloß*) a continuation of politics by other means*. Clausewitz is a *continuation* of Hobbes through other means.

This "simple" continuation is a stabilized unit within the peace / war relationship, from the 18th to the 20th century, up until 1945. But using the word "continuation" might be misleading because it distorts the thought of Clausewitz.

First of all, one must admit that the German language can express certain things that French and English cannot. *Fortsetzung*, which is usually translated as "continuation," is the combination of a dynamic prefix (*Fort*) meaning *departure or surpassing* and a static stem (*Setzung*) evoking a setting in place. It is a word formed of opposites, or rather of a departure and an arrival. The Latinate "continue" does not express the same thing; it is more a continuity than a break: *Cum tenere*, hold together, which makes two static elements in a single word. Clausewitz spoke instead of an active continuity that is more like an extension in the way the work of a disciple is said to extend that of his master. Those who translate his phrase as the "*pursuit* of politics by other means" are closer to the initial meaning. Pursuit, however, combines a dynamic element (*per*, through, beyond) and an active verb (*sequor*, to follow). In fact, as everyone knows, politics in war is much different than politics in peace in both its ends and its means. Clausewitz was well aware of this and decided to use a separate word for political goals (*Zweck*) and for military aims (*Ziel*). The mystery of "continuation" is displaced, set in the atemporal, the diagrammatic: the *Ziel-Zweck* relationship is resolved in the organizational chart of political-military command. It is the old question of the relation between the monarch and commander-in-chief in Sun Zu, of the king—the Prussian staff in Clausewitz—and today between the Pentagon and the Joint Chiefs of Staff.

In any case, this question deserves to be dealt with on an institutional level, but we know that this is not essentially an institutional distinction, rather the difference between two philosophies of action that respond to a philosophical hierarchy. The philosophy of political action must win out over the philosophy of military action, at the risk of the death of democratic sovereignty, which is the internal peace contract.

If the French Army in Algeria had been free to conduct its own war, in other words to decide the Ziel and the Zweck, civil war might have broken out in France, for the Army would have had to constrain the Hexagon to this Zweck, which is the equivalent of a civil war in a democracy. In the end, the French political goal, the acceptance of independence, prevailed.

If the Israeli Army is free to conduct its own war, in other words with no political goal, or fixing its Zweck as the complete submission of the Palestinians or even their expulsion, like a photocopy of the Ziel, or total victory over the Palestinians, it will lead to permanent war, to the destruction of Israeli democracy and to international conflict.

However, we are no longer in this configuration. French Algeria was the objective of another age. A Bantustan Palestine as well. Behind Sharon's excesses lies American military excess, and the abnormal contact between imperial military globality and the absence or dissipation of global diplomacy as transnational politics, its disappearance in the face of a global economy that does not "think politics" but thinks "repression" as a separate sphere, not a continuation but a social mirror of the economy.

The current configuration, in which little wars and the bravado of American military leaders abound, is certainly quite different than the paleo-imperial process of French Algeria; however, the distinction between Ziel and Zweck has become impossible in the global empire because there is no global political power, only a global military power (the American Army) and a global economic power (corporations, the market).

In order to master this complexity without giving up the description of strategies, the principles of decision used by deciding groups, friends or enemies, left or right or on the fence, new words are needed. The Lefts must now place their programs—the fight against inequality and misery and for the extension of sovereignty, culture, civil responsibility and peace to all popular classes—at the global level, already occupied by the Right. Truckloads of goodwill are not enough because the most deadly violence is already at work, not as a continuation of political sovereignty, but as a "continuation" of the global economy by other means without political mediation.

With this goal in mind, I propose a trip through the discourses of Hobbes and Clausewitz to shed light on the problem, though there are certainly other paths that can be explored in practice.

In the two definitions cited above, linked by a sort of conceptual heritage, there are two stages of a pursuit, of a theoretical continuation that binds peace to war and war to peace, sovereignty to the people and the people to sovereignty, democracy to class struggle and class struggle to democracy (instead of Power).

To link Clausewitz and Hobbes, I have deliberately chosen the term "continuation" (thinking of Fortsetzung) to signify as well that their successive contributions to the articulation of war and peace are connected over a long temporal scale: the emergence of disorder and hierarchical medieval violence towards the form of the Nation-State. I move "From Hobbes to Clausewitz and Back," because the decomposition now given shape by the empire resembles a regression to the Middle Ages, a return to the global Behemoth. Of course, it is not a real regression, we have definitively entered human scientific progress, but perhaps we have come into a new configuration where Hobbes' thought can help us understand disorder and its contrary on a global level. But the return to Hobbes, under these conditions, means conserving the concept of the sovereignty of the people and of the social republic, as well as the Clausewitzian baggage.

Clausewitz continues Hobbes in the history of political thought because he accompanies the arrival of popular sovereignty in the republics (or kingdoms) by adjusting the passage from peace to war. This regulation is found in the idea that war can only be explained by a continuation of politics, in other words of sovereignty, by means other than diplomacy. These military means are nonetheless connected to the protection of political sovereignty and not its destruction. The strategic military theory of Clausewitz is based on the structural superiority of defense over offence. A people is better protected by defense than by attacks because defense means "waiting for the enemy's strike" and during this wait, the enemy reveals its plans and risks the morale of its troops, while the defender increases its morale by means of the information on enemy plans that are unveiled and the goal of a defensive war which unites the morale of troops and the people.

In Clausewitzian continuation, one can see an avatar (a reincarnation, a mutation, though fixed and reproducible) of Hobbesian sovereignty built around an implicit contract between the people, refusing the state of war and the Sovereign, an artificial object in charge of managing this contract, like a program written from the bottom up.

This consolidated Hobbesian contract can lead to the distinction between police and standing army (by Guibert and the Count of Saint-Germain) and, certainly, to international Clausewitzian wars.

The continuation of (internal, peaceful) politics by external politics based on potentially violent means was established as a specific task for the Sovereign protector (either the absolute Sovereign-monarch, Sovereign-people or Sovereign-empire). This continuation presupposes an international system in which the notion of equilibrium opposes reaching the extremes of a duel in the climax of an escalation that would be its abstract nature in the isolation of a pure duel. It stops being contradictory after the fall of the Empire of Napoleon with the strategic definition of war by Clausewitz.

One Way / Return Trip

The passage of the state (as a delimited peace by compact) into civil war, as the war of every identity level against all others, is mastered by Hobbes' thought, which explains the emergence of state order, the "Leviathan," while including, by backpedaling, the "Behemoth" scenario whereby this emergence is threatened by military and paramilitary noble revolt.

In France at least, only the Revolution in 1789-1793 brought the insurrection of nobles to an end. Or in any case that role was fulfilled by the 1830 Revolution that cut short the aristocratic reaction of Charles X and brought back the republican colors. In the United States, this only took place with the Civil War. England, starting in 1688, transformed its Behemoth violence into the conquest of a colonial empire (including Ireland). It now seems ready to "sign up" for service with the Empire of Disorder, with the secret hope of organizing it. France, after Napoleon's European imperial episode, found its global imperial vocation much later, though less for conquest than commerce. In the space of a century, it had to conduct two defensive wars on its own territory and lost two wars to re-conquer its empire in Indochina and to defend its conquests in Algeria. It then became a republic again, which is not a defeat but new departure along its original path.

Globalism is now destroying the sovereign function of protection by destroying national sovereignty without building international sovereignty in the form of global protection. The Empire does not act as an international protection (the UN is paralyzed and denied by the US) or as an imperial protection (the Empire both defies and promotes disorder) or as an infranational protection (the sovereignty of *laender* does not have the critical mass needed to confront the sovereignties of global corporations and cannot call on the UN).

How is this connection (continuation-pursuit-*Fortsetzung*) between politics and war expressed in the previous state, in other words, the Hobbesian state? There, civil peace is the continuation of civil war by means of other pacts.

The cycle that dominates Hobbesian thought moves from the sovereign state under compact to Civil War and from Civil War to the sovereign state under compact, and should be read as a circular and diachronic statement of Clausewitzian continuation. Establishing a sovereign, rational state brings the circularity of the civil war-pacified state cycle to an end and inaugurates the distinction between war and politics, though this distinction is not as clear as, nor is it a precise equivalent of, the distinction between war and peace in medieval thought.

Hobbes develops the sequential equality between taking apart, destroying the state and rebuilding it, its construction, through civil war and war. But once the state is built, historically complete, in its struggle against medieval anarchy, and thus once medieval civil war is removed as a threat of Balkanization-Lebanonization disorder inspired by religion, Clausewitz simply considers the continuation between peace and war (between states) as a series of politico-military chronicles that will be called the history of the system of Nations, wars following peace and peace following wars independently of any reformation.

What happens next? How can Clausewitzian continuation be reproduced beyond the (current) destruction of state structures? Will the continuation of politics by other means move to the sub-state level, the level of *laender*, and as a result contribute from below, with imperial support from above, to the destruction of the level of nation-states? The alliance between sub-state and imperial institutions is political, but it is also a war that is being played out in the New World Order of the American imperial monarchy. Since the *laender* will never have a sufficient number of armed forces to confront the transnational Sovereign, politics will be subdivided and made militarily incompetent in the face of economic unification. This incontestable result is what most concerns the "retro-centralizing sovereigntists"—whom I sometimes join on bad days. But the nation itself, which I love and mourn, is not sovereign on the economic level either and can no longer play an autonomous military role in regulating the global Empire. Who are the best allies?

To suggest that the growing asymmetry between the strength of the Empire and republican strength is caused by the electronic revolution is, however, completely up for debate. This asymmetry only grows with the growth of the Empire. But the growth of the Empire can only take place if it maintains an *advance* in air-satellite technology and electronics. If this advance is banalized at each step by the quest for commercial gain, it will be quickly reduced to providing only negligible increases in strength, especially in political terms.

The nanoseconds needed to control targeting and maneuvers in the super-sophisticated jet dogfights of the future are hardly long enough to have serious political weight. Barring a political decision to let the military leadership win, the electronic revolution could become an instrument for logistical equality rather than material inequality (much the same as it was, up to a certain point, for nuclear weapons).

The military strength of the Empire therefore lies essentially in the united weight of the United States, which can reach a supreme power through the systematic warning of their own means (this would be the case even without their cutting-edge technological quality) but this weight is combined with the quality of the hegemony and the alliances technically articulated around the electronic revolution. The electronic revolution in a system looking for commercial profits could just as well be an instrument for software equality rather material inequality (just as nuclear weapons were, up to a certain point). In fact, the electronic revolution allows wars almost without military casualties on America's side, in other words, wars that make it easier to gain political consensus. The more precise tendency would be: wars that need no democratic political consent. Populist media-based consent is enough. However, the areas of virtual alliances, the capacity to form ad hoc coalitions for each imperial expedition, require the global hegemonic framework to be maintained by computerized systems.

Things being what they were at the beginning of the post Cold War era, military asymmetry was already in place in the framework of the bipolar arms race won by the United States. Continuation by other means, by violent means, of the growth of the Empire will practically require it to go back down the steps of the pyramid of escalation: from aerospace-satellite domination to computerized ground forces, then from computerized ground forces to non-lethal police forces; the entire range of means of legitimate transnational violence will go through the imperial organization, which will not be able to keep its system of organization of the technical monopoly of superiority. The Empire should only maintain the monopoly on dominant logistical organization, ensuring the superiority of projective forces, specifically American ones, and the control of the capacity for action of the auxiliaries in domination and the auxiliaries for maintaining order (allies, paramilitaries); in each space-time, degrees of violence are organized: strong arm interventions, peace enforcing missions, forced pacification, policing missions, humanitarian missions. A unified range of war-peace means. Imperial computerized violence is by definition superior to both the state and sub-state (*laender*) level by controlling the brief time of the targeted menace, be it financial or military, and also by the choice, which always remains open, between dominating by using states against the *laender* or the *laender* against states, with the help of multinational corporations. It is somewhat like former times when the king ruled by relying on the nobility against the people or the people against the nobles with the help of the clergy.

Corporations, however, are not the clergy, and rid themselves of any protective role determined by laws or ethics, in the great move towards freedom in firing that has dominated the corporate concentrations for many years. What remains is the flight of the vanquished into hostage taking, delinquency and barbaric violence. Whence the need for a world war against terrorism.

Death and Transfiguration

In practice, the Clausewitzian garden seems destroyed. The compromise on a national level allowing a distinction between peace and war and their unity in the political continuation of a nation-state outside its borders supposes pacific local management of class struggle through equitable distribution of revenues, and its armistice founds the state. This view has become provincial. Both paleo-Jacobins and neo-Girondins are trying to define socio-economic identities on too small a scale. Paleo-Jacobins defend a strong political level, but one that is too economically restrictive. The neo-Girondins, on the side of the *regions*, aim in France to dismantle both national sovereignty and the nascent European sovereignty. The situation is different in Germany where the strong political identities are defined by the *laender* and where, as a consequence, politics can take on an anti-global identity. The differences between these two nations should not lead to a single formulation of the modalities of identity resistance to globalization. By seeking to federalize France so it resembles Germany in order to combine the two more easily, the neo-Girondins follow a "neo-Jacobin European" dogmatism: does European unity have to emerge from uniformity? The vision defended by Helmut Kohl of a "Europe of *laender*" was influenced by the stereotypical attitude of Jacobins in the Empire who proclaim the global virtues of French departments.

How can one really give an account of what the state and popular sovereignty become when frontiers disappear, frontiers that formed semi-porous compartments of class struggle and politics, allowing the state to organize its monopoly on legitimate violence by distinguishing between interior police actions and exterior military logic? What are the interior and exterior of a sovereign entity that is no longer primarily formed of peasant lands and fields, but of a territory occupied by co-inhabitants and neighbors, and that is trying to manage an "exterior" that is no longer geographic?

Is there a continuation of politics by other means than war, or a narrow representation of the state? Is globalism inherently violent and apolitical, i.e. bent on destroying popular sovereignty?

4. Violence and Globalism[29]

In strategy, the word "globalism" should have a partisan definition: "doctrine, ideology or strategy *favorable* to globality." Globality qualifies a phenomenon that covers the globe. And globalists are those who defend globalism. This idea can make sense economically (global enterprise, single market) or religiously (the "Catholic" church—reigning over everything, one god; Islam, one peace) and is valid for electromagnetic communication as well as satellite observation. For democracy, however, it is meaningless. Democracy, no, by no means.

Excluding ecology, necessary ecumenical, I am not in the least favorable to any economic or political phenomenon being extended to the entire globe, except, perhaps, certain elementary ideas like liberty, equality and fraternity, in terms of nutrition, education and expression. Freedom of expression naturally leads to diversity. Equality in instruction raises countless problems and supposes an infinite variety of approaches for each culture and each child. Fraternity in nutrition is obviously not a question of quantity; however, it seems unlikely that this will ever become a "global function," even during periods of abundance, given the myriad variety of cuisine in the world and the resistance offered by certain types of cuisine (African, Arab, Chinese, French, Indian, Peruvian, etc.) to the "global" cuisine promoted in the United States.

True globality is thus only present today in three areas: the *financial* sphere on the one hand; the *military* sector on the other; the sphere of electromagnetic *communications*, which, in its search for real time, must rely on both the military and financial.

This odd Trinity merits reflection (the Father a financier, the Son a soldier and the Holy Ghost an electromagnetic dependant of Father and Son). It does not establish the Republic of Plato on the universal level. Nor does it establish the reign of the Christian Trinity. In economy and politics, there are no global philosophies. But finance is not the economy. The Web is not the Holy Spirit or Wisdom. Only the warriors of the Republic of Plato are in place, but they are being privatized, recruited and commanded like mercenaries, and are therefore a far cry from the pure Lycurgean model that inspired Plato. Military America resembles 4th century Sparta, producing soldiers and exporting mercenaries privately. And it is not the only one.

Of course, the globality of a phenomenon is not only, or not necessarily, determined by domination, polarity or strategy; it can also be an unwanted effect of the communication revolution, a reduction in hierarchical structures through a network of horizontal human relationships and universal friendship. This ideal is still only a dream (one marked by the Internet boom) and hierarchies are being recreated on the worldwide "web."

The above terms are borrowed from theoretical strategy, which is not only an instrument for correctly conducting wars, but can also serve to provide a better explanation of human combat and *critique,* the models that have rationalized the use of armed violence and death threats ever since the Neolithic era as a way to save lives. Violent political behavior can be logical and even mathematical, but the representations and fundamental beliefs that underlie the logical use of violence can also be completely revolting. The racism inherent in the Nazi superman, for example. Or the unalterable imperatives of major religions. That is why there is no pure strategy. There is just *strategy* as a critical approach and the more sovereign *politics,* which can often take a turn for the worst.

The Strategic Approach

The strategic approach is an interdisciplinary approach with a defined object: the *rational decisions* made in the name of collective identities *in the sphere of danger* and even under the threat of death.

Traditionally, there were two types of death threats that could attain members of a group: the threat of death by *arms,* or death by *starvation* arising from either a natural disaster (drought, flooding) or an aggressive human action (blockade, siege, destruction of harvests). These two threats underlie the constitution of the state as a system, function or contract of "protection." More recently, the threat of "artificial disasters," stock market crashes or rampant inflation, for example, has emerged. They are called "artificial" in recognition of the difference, already present in Aristotle, between *oeconomia*, the natural means of survival (*oiko-nomia*, regulation of a household as an agricultural or trade unit of production), and *chrematistic* means, the artificial means of acquiring goods, techniques of using revenue that include usury and speculative monetary transactions without creating natural riches. An artificial disaster is a chrematistic one.

The term strategy referred primarily to the major military decisions taken on a national level or concerning the behavior of an entire army (*Stratos*, the army; *Hegeia*, behavior). Strategy could not be considered without also taking tactics into consideration, which call on the more technical art of subordinate officers and soldiers to deal with the geometry of deployment and the efficient distribution of weapons.

But we now have the idea that there is *strategy* on the one hand, the political-operational dialectic, and *tactics* on the other, the technical-operational dialectic, in each possible type of military conflict. There would thus be strategy and tactics at the level of the theater of operations as well as at the level of the combatants. Moreover, it is possible to consider the existence of death threats at every level of human organization. If it is admitted that the death of a collective does not necessarily imply the death of its members but their "de-membering," then political conservation of identities relies on strategy whereas the military conservation of combat units depends on tactics. *At the very limit*, it could be said that the preservation of an individual as a political identity is a strategic activity, while the preservation of the life of a soldier as an individual body, the smallest military unit in combat, is both tactical and strategic.

Today, one must recognize that when faced with different types of threats, identities can act strategically—and not solely tactically—at every level of human organization. General Lucien Poirier reminds us of this in his book, *The Strategic Workshop*,[30] a sort of Platonic dialogue orchestrated by Gérard Chaliand. By adding to his toolbox the concept of *scale invariance*, borrowed from the realm of fractal objects, he notes that "at every level of the politico-strategic structure, from the politician to the individual soldier, each agent makes use of all categories" of strategy and that "strategic thinking is not a privilege, as was once thought, of the upper echelons of calculation and decision making."

Poirier dismantles in passing bygone representations of military hierarchy and even of social hierarchy. And, despite himself perhaps, he repositions democracy *within theoretical strategy*, in other words the sovereignty of the people, as an investment in the universal strategic competency of democratic citizens.

Preventing Civil War

As members of a sovereign population, democratic citizens enter into confrontation for the common good, using these peaceful battles to control the violence that hovers on the brink of an ever possible civil war.

Strategy, present on every level, gives constitutions their form. But to complete this examination of the current extension of the word "strategy," it must be noted that there is no reason to believe that strategy only has one object, war and victory over others. Nor that this confrontation is a game that adds up to nothing. Ever since Ancient Greece, democracy and the civil war it suspends within the city-state only have one strategic object: the peaceful distribution of goods, including symbolic goods, between rich and poor. Aristotle states this very clearly. This distribution is not a game that adds up to nothing, even in ancient times, without an increase in production expected from "progress," for the city-state can engage in profitable wars and share the spoils in a way that represents the beginnings of an equitable distribution of well-being. Also because internal peace is itself a common good, a pledge of productivity and well-being, and its preservation can be, at times, the primary common objective for both rich and poor, especially when threatened from the outside. The existence of a middle class *encourages*, but does not embody, according to Aristotle, the preservation of peace. In attempting to maintain its standard of living, the middle class can be more ferocious than the rich who have deeper pockets. Plato, a greater admirer of the Spartan regime than Aristotle, thought he could maintain concord *(homonia)* by imagining three castes: a superior caste made up of philosophers; a lower one responsible for producing basic goods; and a middle class as an internal-external rampart of the city-state, a caste of warriors directly responsible for maintaining peace through force, and not a intermediary aristocracy that would maintain harmony through moderation.

Whatever the case may be, ancient democracy (including the suspended civil war) only took practical form in the closed field of an electoral circumscription or a group of circumscriptions where a common means of counting citizen's points or votes in the regulated conflicts of elections had been accepted. In other words, *Greek democracy must be seen as a combat sport*, in the same way, perhaps, that a well-regulated *hoplitic battle*, opposing ranks of equal citizens against each other in the harsh combat of the front lines, *could be seen as a bloody election*, establishing a hierarchy of city-states.

In the mindset of the Greek city-state, which is closer to our own than one might think, the suspension of civil war by means of democracy always required the *delimitation of the city-state* in order to count votes and to measure the consensus on adjusting or regulating the inequality between the rich and the poor. Democratic consensus can only apply within the boundaries of the city-state. It would be meaningless, or even unthinkable, to make decisions about the redistribution of wealth in neighboring areas, unless one was considering to appropriate it for oneself. Internal democracy and peaceful internal relations do not imply a peaceful relationship with the *outside*, especially if the city-state accepts slavery and sees the enslavement of prisoners as a means of absorbing the costs of victory and creating harmony between rich and poor once the external danger that united them has disappeared. But what remains of this little local project in an *Empire* and, from now on, in the *globality*?

The Birth of Predatory Empires

Maneuvering to maintain harmony between rich and poor through redistribution or predatory practices does not only involve "city-states," but also the strategic center of Empires, aggregates of city-states (republics or kingdoms) established under military hegemony. There are three instances of Empire formation in "Western History" alone:

1. The Sumerian and Akkad empires and their successors (Babylonian, Assyrian, Mede, Persian) emerging from the constellation of Neolithic towns.

2. Alexander's Empire emerging from the constellation of Greek city-states, most of which allowed slavery. It was followed by the Roman Empire, then Byzantium, the Sultanate, the Ottoman Empire and the Russian Empire.

3. The development of predatory colonial empires during the 16th-18th centuries and the accumulation that is at the source of the modern capitalist system, emerging from the constellation of European merchant cities (Hanseatic, German, Italian) and bourgeois support for conquering monarchies (Portugal, Catalonia, Spain, Holland, Great Britain).

From a strategic standpoint, these three moments of empire formation follow two main patterns in the founding of the imperial state. The first proceeds from a vision of the economy as a globality, which I call the *logistical* empire; and the second, the *predatory* empire, from the emergence of violent conquest as a rational economic factor.

In the "logistical state" (Sumeria, Egypt, Etruscan Rome), religion becomes a means of supervising humanized nature by *eliminating wastefulness*, regulating the use of water and *controlling the seasons*. The state grows and spreads. It spreads more on the strength of its reserves and the flows of consumer goods, which are its weapons of harmony and of shared well-being, than by the use of arms and the power of invasion. In the logistical state, the *economy dominates violence because violence can be bought*. The major medieval orders (even including the Jesuits, admirers of the great Oriental civilizations) always tried to recreate logistical societies based on work in the form of local micro-activities combined into networks, but also on the rational exploitation of nature. Economy was conceived as an autonomous sphere of reason, *creating* its territories, purchasing its safety with both financial power and the manipulation of sacred threats.

Yet the stable wealth of the "Oriental" logistical order attracted predatory actions from the very beginning.

The birth of the predatory, conquering state (Akkad, Assyrian Empire, Latin Rome, etc.) lies in the temptation presented by the commerce and reserves of the logistical state. Restructured by its invaders or recently civilized (though still predatory, barbarians) the state organizes through violence a part of the accumulated surplus. The predatory empire spreads by means of invasion and violent domination. The "inflatable" imperial conglomerates that it establishes are more or less durable in a subtle hierarchy of societies conquered from the center to the periphery, each of which is subjected to a different level of predatory imposition. In the predatory empire, *violence dominates the economy because it can expand it by means of expeditionary invasions and forced accumulation.*

Geopolitics of Fear

But an excess of wealth can weaken military defenses and an excess of expertise in violence can devastate the economy in the long run; a new temporality is imposed on these empires, a more historical time that presents itself as cyclical. In the European theater, the predatory center moves from East to West in a fish scale progression, starting from the Mesopotamian cradle of the state. It is a commonplace, first in the Bible, then in Greek historiography to speak of the *succession* of predatory empires and their migration to the West. We could also suggest the migration of logistical empires to the East, in India and China.

As economic machines normally producing negentropy (order, internal peace, wealth), these systems cannot last eternally; the pre-industrial predatory Empire works like a clock carefully wound with all the skill of keeping the goose with golden eggs alive. It increases its survival time either by returning to a moderate logistical system, or by pursuing its foreign predatory conquests at the risk of military *surfeit*, an over-developed specialization towards specific end (τελος): in this case, perfecting destructive military capabilities at the expense of productive, economic capabilities. This over-development can take two forms, either an internal redistribution of the spoils at the risk of exhausting all the reserves, or a decentralization producing management economies with a reduction of privileged bureaucracies, at the risk of Balkanization of military sovereignty by means of wars of liberation or less predatory invasions.

But these ways of prolonging the life of an empire are also methods of self-destruction. The longest imperial experiment, the Chinese Empire, went through many cycles of logistical empires, barbarian invasions and separation into more or less predatory kingdoms without losing its identity as the *Middle Empire* (*Tchung Kuo*), or moving its center without losing sight of the historical continuity of China. In the West, however, the Roman, Byzantine and Carolingian Empires, the sultanates, the Holy Roman Empire, Tsarism, Napoleon, the British Empire, the French colonial Empire and Hitler have disappeared forever. Europe is a recent political construct.

The transformation of the Russian empire and the materialization of the American empire, opposed like the two halves of the world, tracing a fortified boundary across the territory of a divided Europe, shows that a predatory imperial form prefers seeking out confrontation with an Other and an outside, and in this way it can never become global.

Europe as an identity organizing internal peace is a recent political expression, just as America is a recent empire. The recent designation (in May 2000) of China as a virtual main rival (*peer competitor*) of the American empire, the designation in 2001 of "Islamic terrorism" as a global enemy, the designation once again of three states—North Korea, Iran and Iraq—as "rogue states" for the mere fact that they are accused of trying to develop nuclear weapons, shows that the single Empire is looking for both the unity and plurality that will allow it to keep a predatory relationship with an exterior. It is concerned that unifying world imperial power (the mon-archy, to borrow Dante's vocabulary) would require it to base its power throughout the world on internal global violence or to establish Universal Peace without predatory oppression, an even more paradoxical task.

The American Empire is thus faced with a traditional problem. By perfecting the predatory and repressive military machine to the extreme, which could become necessary to its reproduction, the Empire could veer towards a monstrous overdevelopment of the destructive, or merely repressive, function of the state, threatening its subjects with death. The "people" always decide the end of logistical-predatory empires through various forms of plebian secession, of anachoresis[31] or of invasions greeted as liberations. There is a type of collapse without invasion exemplified by the fall of the Assyrian Empire.

A giant with clay feet, built on the mud of Mesopotamian irrigation, on the over-exploitation of Neolithic techniques, without any progress in productivity, save in techniques of destruction, Assyrian militarism disappeared all at once, *just like, I might add, the Soviet Empire*, caught in the breathless arms race orchestrated by the United States.

Modern Imperialism

The relation between economy and violence, however, has changed drastically with the beginning of the accumulation of capital and the scientific development of technology. Which system of domination prevails in the modern Empire-states, and ultimately in the American Empire?

As the economy reached a global scale, in the 16th century, and violence was still clearly regional, the question of combining the governmental organization of regional Empires and the workings of the global economy—what Braudel and Wallerstein call *world-*

economy and its relationship to the world-Empire[32]—returns to the opposition already prevalent between logistical Empires and predatory Empires at the dawn of the Classical era:

If, as Braudel claims, mercantile economy (in particular the Portuguese adventure, the first global expedition) is the management of the local "contact between two desires," this contact, this logic of desire transgresses military boundaries, even if the flows are sometimes momentarily interrupted by vandals and pirates.

The economy is capable of shaping violence because it can break through or circumvent military barriers, especially on the ocean where it is easier to escape than on a road. The economy can force its way through military barriers on land or in ports, making them "porous" with the smell of profits. Armed men alternatively consider this profit to be either a corruption of discipline or as the prerogative of the strong (through ransom, rackets). They may therefore be manipulated.

But it is also true that the regulated deployment of military violence, or merely the threat of violence suffices to form the equivalent of canals and dikes to control the flow of economic flux: it establishes necessary rules. *Violence can shape the economy*.

Looking back at the history of Empires can help us understand the current crisis in democracy. It appears triumphant, while in fact the disparity between rich and poor is growing across the globe. Something resembling global structural slavery has reappeared, leaving us with the prospect of Spartan cities with *hilotes,* or totalitarian empires with camps and slavery.

The only benefit of the globalization of finance and military force for humanity is that it obliges us to *think of a global means of equitable distribution*, which is the only way to avoid the worldwide civil war that threatens to take the form of cold, barbaric violence.

The structures for reception and hospitality, which alone found the market, remain the fixed points of the new networks. But at the next stage, the specialized war fleets of the West police the seas and suddenly become the masters of distant flux, in a way that the merchants and minor kings of coastal Asia could not have foreseen.

The predatory behavior and intense parasiting of the economies and commerce from India to the Indies that was necessary for the primitive development of European capital were above all built around the invention of the war ship, bursting with canons and not directly in charge of carrying out predatory activities but rather of preventing violent local exaction.

In the history of the 18th to the 20th centuries, the truly mercantile maritime empires (British) favored a logistical formula, while the conquering, land-based empires (Spanish, French) preferred the predatory formula. In fact, each was both predatory and logistical; however, the maritime empires were predators attached to fluxes whereas the land-based empires would parasite stocks (reserves of men, land, minerals). The Spanish empire was more logistical in the peasant enclaves of the grand, pre-Hispanic logistical empires (Andes, Mexico) and more predatory in the exploitation of African slaves for sugar production elsewhere. The British empire was both terrestrial and logistical in India.

The Americans first became land-based and predatory in America, though they were called "pioneers" in the sense that they took lands by chasing people out or forcing them to submit, which is a nuance in the predatory activity the also characterizes Zionism and early South Africa. All of the examples, these beginning scenarios, these cases must be kept in mind in order to examine in contemporary cases at what level the economy definitively determines violence, at what level violence directs the economy. The problem is a current one since the absolute preeminence of the economy is the tireless refrain of the neo-liberals who shape the globalist ideology. Given the configuration of the 21st century American Empire: has the economy won out over violence and does the Empire work like a logistical empire, not by making good soldiers but especially by making good weapons with money; or has violence won out over the economy and does the Empire work like a predatory empire making money with good soldiers?

Or is it more appropriate to say that the question can no longer be asked in the same way due to the robotization of violence?

Obviously, global balance would mean the end of capitalism. A scholastic problem that has nonetheless never ceased to be considered by brief periods since the birth of capitalism.

The "End of Capitalism," an Academic Question

Stability of the Empire comes from the "perfect" equivalence between the organized form of military violence and the organized form of the economy. This perfect equivalence has left unforgettable moments, like the *pax romana*, a fragile moment of equilibrium under the Antonins that was dreamt of as the harmony of the world. But this sort of perfection is not of this world. The cruise ship regime of the Empire is always based on exaction. Stability encounters particular difficulties during the globalization phase that should be defined from this angle to expose the places where its perfection can be opposed. This concern accompanies capitalism from its birth as a worldwide system. But making the forms of violence and of the economy compatible in a stable way would certainly be the end of capitalism, though not necessarily a paradise.

5. Strategic Future

At this point in the review of the levels, risks and rules of the intra-state and inter-imperial conflict, the strategic problem of economic and military globality in the face of the democratic ideal, introduces the question of whether violence can take hold of the entire globe, whether peace and democracy will occupy this position, or whether a median position between the two will arise. History hesitates between these two poles and the form it takes in our lifetime, should be examined now that the globe is almost completely unified under the imperial power of the United States—at least as a *representation*.

Can principles of cosmopolitan rights be formulated that would avoid diffuse, "constant war"? Let us turn to a quote from Immanuel Kant, who saw the circular shape of the earth as an abstract form that would inevitably lead to universal peace: "The alien […] may request the right to be *a permanent visitor* (it would require a special, charitable agreement to make him a fellow inhabitant for a certain period), but the *right to visit*, to associate, belongs to all men by virtue of their common ownership of the earth's surface; for since the earth is a globe, they cannot scatter infinitely, but must, finally, tolerate living in close proximity."[33]

Or should we, on the contrary, agree with Fichte, for whom a *realpolitk* should aim to "unite the politics of international power and internal dictatorship after the world is conquered by a single sovereign, the only means of ensuring universal peace."[34]

Overwhelmed by the size of this last problem, which is still relevant today, and by the apparent naiveté its formulation, I will begin with a few definitions that will allow me to treat these questions in succession.

What Political Globalisation?

A brief strategic history of the world: state violence is a *formal* violence establishing the division between interior and exterior; it bases civil peace on external wars. War siphons violence away from class struggle by means of conflict between states. The isolated Empires that first emerge in the midst of barbarians end up being neighbors as a result of their conquests. Instead of constellations of globalities with no systemic contact (China, Roman Empire), a global system of imperial systems interconnected by their colonial conquests is formed, followed by the World Wars and the bipolarization of the Cold War. This stand-off disappeared in 1989, ending in a *renovatio mundi* ceremoniously proclaimed by President Bush on the eve of the Gulf War.

The specificity of the current historical situation is dependent on the following phenomenon: after the long history of Universal Empires, each of which considered itself to be in the *middle* of the newly discovered lands around it and claimed mastery over the "four corners" of the earth, the term globality now, for the first time, actually encompasses the entire globe and all of humankind (at least as a *technical representation*).

The notion of globality presupposes an enclosed *space* considered as a whole. An island or a planet are natural globalities. Like Vidal de la Blache, I reject the tendency to legitimate representations of globality in terms of land and prefer human geography to geopolitics.[35] I also reject any principle of hierarchical segmentation of the "human race" as well as any apotheosis of religious differences as exclusive global identities. Making such a "Huntingtonian choice" would provide a legitimate framework for interethnic conflicts and I have neither the intention nor the need to engage in discussion with those who rely on this type of representation. By their own definition they are the theoretical and political enemies I am actively trying to defeat. War between segmented and peripheral communities is actually the way they theorize how the central peace of masters of Empires is ensured thanks to the foolish religious quarrels between poor assassins.

As a Frenchman, or more precisely as a Breton from my father's side, Jewish from my mother's side, Latin-American through my wife and children, North African through my childhood and Greek by my religion, a adoptive resident of Burgundy and Parisian by birth, I do not have to uphold the imperial representation that would oblige me to wage war against myself. It is the opposite of the universal social republic. And I am not alone in that.

I prefer to speak of the "human geography" rather than the "geopolitics" of communities and assert that this "global" political space is necessarily geographic, at least as far as its *inhabitants* are concerned, people linked to an ecological territory who attempt to survive in a friendly way and without ceaseless nomadism. In strategic terms, *globality* does not necessarily apply to societal identities but always applies to two spheres of human survival:

- the economic sphere (production, logistics, market, consumption)
- the violent sphere (conquest, predatory actions, domination, destruction)

Politics is precisely defined here as the space where the relationship between violence and economy is managed practically.

One of the general *strategic* problems, perhaps the most general one, should be to determine how these two globalities that sometimes coincide, intersect and overlap are co-extensive; how more often than not they are coordinated, linked, in contact without perfectly coinciding; in short, it is necessary to determine how these two spheres organize and counteract each other, how they join or separate within the unstable, often ephemeral but always *composite* systems of political sovereignty.

Taken in this sense, politics cannot disappear by imperial decree. Can it be global? More precisely, two questions need to be asked:

- Has the United States given itself the means to function as dominant global imperial political institution?
- Should this institution be the UN instead?

Any other solution would mean the absence of global politics. But this still does not tell us what scale is the most pertinent for controlling globalizing imperial political structures. Before treating that problem, we should first ask whether the unifying *virtù* of the Americans is truly economic, as they say it is, or whether it is not, despite what they claim, fundamentally military. The answer can be found in the details, in their practices, rather than in their declarations.

We should also ask, setting aside American practices—for even if they are dominant, they are not the only ones around—by which of the two globalities, economic or military, the earth tends to be unified.

Is it simply a question of economic unification through the

markets? Or only the financial markets? Or is it on the contrary simply a question of unification through the latent violence of the ubiquitous military system of the United States? Or of the NATO system that can be distinguished from it? Or the Euro-Atlantic system, at an even more general level?

Or if it is unified *politically* by an active, constant, legitimate mediation between economic and military criteria carried out by governments and to a certain extent under the influence of their citizens (an agile, organized influence, capable of *targeting* certain concerns with an *acentral* movement, through the global effects of the Net and the media)?

The New Post-Cold War Globality

The strategic question of whether the domination established by the United States over the planet is above all economic or military remains open, and the response will define how we conceive of the future. The question of the role of religion in the strategic shaping of the world today should also be seriously considered. There are five different realities possible concerning the form of imperfect strategic globality that has reigned since the Gulf War. I will list them first before treating each one separately:

1. The Domination of military globality over economic globality: predatory peace
2. Imperial substitutes for wars of conquest
3. Micro-military "national" compensation for macro-economic globalization: internal wars
4. Conformity established between the violent and economic means through computerization (secrecy, real time, precise targeting)
5. The Empire turns religious?

1. The Domination of military globality over economic globality: predatory peace

The elimination of the Berlin wall and the Iron Curtain produced the first real globality in history, but it was a military event that created a military globality, rather than an economic one at first.

In fact, two negative moments from a military perspective marked the period: a wall falling without a fight (Berlin), Soviet abstention from a war in their glacis (the Gulf War). These two events sealed the defeat of the Soviet economic system and the Soviet military. There can be no economic defeat in a global Empire without a military defeat. Not necessarily a defeat during a wartime operation: a mixed defeat, both economic and military, in the arms race occurred in the East and a political collapse was then enough to finish it.

At this turning point, Fukuyama was premature in declaring the "End of History"[36] because globality, the formation of a truly global world economy, is not as easy as it seems. It runs up against the presence of politico-military sovereignties maintaining spaces that prevent total market economy unification. A few states still consider themselves Marxist (China, Vietnam, Korea, Cuba), some states still maintain a partially controlled economy, either by vocation or due to a prolonged state of war (Iraq, Iran, Serbia). Other states have preserved a large nationalized sector, and even the ideology behind the nationalization of major public services and public works projects by the state. Even capitalist Europe calls for a *social* market economy and supports the need for sovereign regulations of the economy.

More theoretically speaking, the dogmatic defenders of the free-market economy cannot prove that free-market institutions can arise without rules, without the state acting as a guarantor of its political will, imposing the suspension of predatory violence at the gates of the marketplace or, better yet, of the entire nation.

The "predatory peace" proclaimed after the military victory of the American Empire in the name of the universal free-market ideology, imposed the representation of an economic globality that did not yet exist. The end of violence in the world bazaar cannot yet be regulated by a world state—which neither exists nor is desired by the United States—or better yet, local states, which lack the competence. Any regulation in the meantime must be done partially and empirically through negotiations that remain confidential between violent Mafias and unarmed Merchants.

Predatory peace is only a virtual paradigm with value for an improbable future and not for the present. It is not a stable state, but a process; in American strategic vocabulary, it is called *enlargement*, the extension of democracy *and* free-market economy to the entire globe. Announced by Anthony Lake in 1993, enlargement will *end* (so they say) in economic globality, if the future prophecy goes according to Clintonian plans and market enlargement produces its own profitability.

2. Imperial substitutes for wars of conquest

However, the Cold War of the Empire against an enemy or another (barbarian) Empire no longer exists to siphon the contradictions of class struggle away from the Empire through populist-style mobilizations. The American Empire must face the strategic problem in the traditional form that all Empires had to face if, like the Roman or Chinese Empires, they considered themselves to be "alone in the world," since they knew nothing about the others. The competing colonial Empires had to face the same problem: class struggles are traditionally "drained off" by delimiting a space to conquer. But what happens if conquest is no longer profitable in the "barbarian areas" (Rome gave up trying to conquer

Germania) or if there are no more "barbarian areas"? There are two abstract strategies that were applied both in the history of the Roman Empire as in the history of European colonial empires:

a) The Empire can *recreate a military enemy within the economic globality* to polarize itself and suspend class struggle in the name of security with repressive wars. This exterior is "naturally" present: it includes zones of poverty that do not form a "market" and can therefore become *purely military* marches again. Internal war in zones of poverty. One could say that it is taking shape in the United States.

b) The Empire can also *reauthorize war within the newly drawn globality of military leadership in order to redefine peace.*

War is illegitimate and hindered in the world today by two obstacles that are beneficial in principle, but do not really work to prohibit war. Authorizing international wars is within the grasp of the military leadership of the United States. The return of local duels has been facilitated by the removal of two hindrances:

- war is hindered by the prohibition on international wars by the UN; it is the equivalent of a police prohibition on duels within a unified world. The UN Security Council would be in charge of the policing function of the World Empire. This is the project on which the UN institution was built—at least on paper. A UN General Staff has nonetheless never been formed, much less a specifically UN military force. There are no archers on watch under the orders of the king. This model does not work. The UN at most plays the role of a weakened papacy.

- war is theoretically hindered by the United States itself, the global imperial military nation, with its own doctrine of military intervention: *Zero GI casualties* and the reshaping of NATO into its new role of sending out forces that no longer have anything to do with defending against the USSR, causing a crisis in alliances and representations.

Outlawing duels in the 17th century presupposed a project for definitive and legitimate pacification imposed by modern states. The UN is not a state and the United States at the head of a new type of Empire does not wish to conquer or pacify the world. The prevalence of local duels is growing before our very eyes. Wars today are tearing states to shreds throughout the world.

The second hindrance (zero American casualties and no conquest) in fact paralyzes or cancels out the first (UN intervention in the name of principles).

3. Micro-military "national" compensation for macro-economic globalization: internal wars

The risk of armed conflict today depends more on the fault lines within states than armed conflict between states. This reality has become more evident in the Mediterranean basin after the wars in ex-Yugoslavia, the breakdown of Albania and the Algerian implosion. The Israeli-Palestinian conflict now suddenly appears for what it is since the end of the Mandate: a South-African type of post-colonial social conflict between communities. A part of "globalization" accepts the pulverization of political identities and allows wounds to remain open; it therefore accepts Balkanization as a general law. I will come back to this point in greater detail when discussing Balkanized wars.

4. Conformity established between the violent and economic means through computerization (secrecy, real time, precise targeting)

It is now indispensable for the United States to unite, to globalize markets. In order to do so, certain strategic schools consider it *therefore* necessary to unite-globalize the violent institutions of military and police repression and peace missions, so as to *make virtual violence conform to the global economic system.* (It is "smoothed over" by the fluid tissue of multinational corporations, in conformity with the undifferentiated space-time of world markets). This model for the globalization of violence no longer seeks to imitate the model of the commercial market—the archaic object that can only be described as a bulky logistical command performing guard services and vice squad duty—but the model of the *delocalized real time* of the financial market through an acentral transformation.

The problem of the *reality* of this change for the United States space is not only speculative; they also want it to be operative and prescriptive. It *must* be made to happen. The American elite pursues this objective with pioneering zeal supported by immense religious representations based on the Bible. They also need the global economy to be buttressed by a subtle global *organization* (ubiquitous, punitive, measured, with zero tolerance) of imperial violence, the only one that can manifest and implement the justice of their Empire in the eyes of history. The religious model fits perfectly.

5. The Empire turns religious?

I invite economists and strategists to take religious representations in the new imperial globality seriously. At least as much as Stalinist ideology, American politics and civilization could be considered as a monotheistic heresy proclaiming the kingdom of God on earth, and therefore more a Muslim or Jewish heresy than a Christian one. The Sunnite Islam of the oil monarchies and republics, Judaism in its archaic or modern forms, Protestantism since the dawn of capitalism according to Weber, the papacy by crushing the theology of freedom, the Orthodox church by adoring almost every Tsar—all the major religions seem to have contributed to the triumph of this heresy. It is truly a fourth religion of the Book. They need their project to have populist support, even if it comes from stateless populism, and the change, as a deliberate strategy, seeks help from vast religious representations, and not just advertising.

For reasons of strategic coherence, the global economy must be supported by a global *organization* of violence and vice versa. This coherence through religiousness is the only one that can make the *justice* of the Empire historically manifest, whereas the law of the market left alone leads to injustice. The papacy must cast a grim eye on this attempt. It has witnessed many more for the last two-thousand years.

But we are not here to condemn heresies; in the name of what orthodoxy would we speak? A heresy is always an extreme mani-festation of religiousness. We must analyze this phenomenon with ordinary political concepts, but also with the anthropologi-cal, poetic and shamanistic attention it deserves.

The critical cases in Somalia, Rwanda, Chechnya, the Kurds, Azeri-Armenians, in Georgia, Mexico, Colombia, Peru, Belgium, the Montana militias and the mad bombers in Oklahoma reveal that decomposition into ethnic-religious-political sub-groups is not limited to the "South" alone, or that there is a South in the North.

In conclusion, *sub-state violence does seem to be the result of a current global logic, and not of a "local archaism," which does exists, but only to give a specific form to local violence.*

The "weight of history" argument is the laziest of excuses for strategic irresponsibility. French politics shamefully relied on it in the Balkans when Yugoslavian disintegration began. The Americans also have the tendency to fall back on this "objective" observation when they do not want to take sides assuming that the "sides" involved in these conflicts are archaic political neuroses.

These archaic political neuroses also exist in the "overdeveloped center of the planet." Some find the archaic and cruel Serbian militias *sympathetic* despite their crimes because they are waging a hopeless war against the steam-roller of modern Euro-Atlantic capitalism. In sympathy, there is *common suffering*. An extreme danger that one should not observe with the disdain of the masters of contentment. How can these wounds be prevented or healed? By taking sides, and not at a distance.

The Global Causes of Current Conflicts

However illegitimate it may be, war has not disappeared from the face of the globe. It thrives despite the prohibition of a militarily powerless UN and thanks to the American doctrine of "zero casualty" military intervention (it obliges them to intervene only when the war has run its course, preferably with the reciprocal massacre of the trouble-makers). As a result, peace comes slowly.

Class conflict has not disappeared, but has made a prodigious, disconcerting leap since it should now be inscribed at a global level: the globalization of the economy makes it difficult to identify the dominant classes and brings an end to their association with sectors of the subjugated classes that remain local or national. Laws no longer codify class relations except at the tactical level of local political concerns. The "social guarantee" Condorcet included in his February 15, 1793 project for a new social compact can no longer be extended on a national scale. At the time the Montagnards thought the law would not be able to ensure anything and that *the right of popular revolt was the only serious guarantee of the social compact*. The right to revolt ensured a balance of local power. It was the equivalent of a pact. This right has lost its hold under global relationships of power and the global compact has lost its form ever since. The disintegration of the USSR prevents the regulation of the worldwide class struggle, even through the myth of the "Socialist homeland."

Systems for "siphoning disorder" at a larger or smaller scale than the state *therefore* tend to be recreated. It is in the interests of the ill-defined global aristocracy that manages global social fractures (between the American Senate, Mafia, European banks, IMF), to attempt to maintain the local identities of protection or revolt that have stupidly developed everywhere. The Huntingtonian paradigm of confrontation between civilizations legitimizes forms of identity that are locally incapable of strategically identify real stakes.

The "fundamentalist religious" form of the Peoples of the Book is the most effective illusion of identity, because it remains strategically open on the globe and thus joins the reigning global, financial, transnational identity. The United States promotes Islam, even fundamentalist Islam, through Saudia Arabia and Pakistan, as well as fundamentalist Judaism and Baptism: these religious instruments promote an archaic destruction of secular nation-states, but with the caravan-travelling, merchant mind-set of major pilgrimages and international brotherhoods, they also play a role in the future macro-strategic representation of the global reunification of markets.

At the same time, they promote sectarian, "racist" or nationalist forms, autistic and negentropic identities that can turn zones with little to no global economic interest into "failed states" and areas of self-extermination.

The Hellish Descent

With their backwards representations of world reality, certain defenders of community identities experience Balkanization as a sort of liberation, and then can continue their descent to Lebanonization to the point of diced identities: neighborhoods, clans, families. Taken to the extreme, sects or individuals themselves go "insane," Lebanonizing themselves, then committing suicide after a massacre. Identity sub-systems, in their hellish descent, end up with the entropy they hoped to avoid, unless someone intervenes, not necessarily from outside their territory, but from outside the system of entropy. Intervention presupposes the creation of a branch of political science considered in its statutes to be a curative practice, while diagnosis and treatment would become rational methods of seeking peace.

But who would support this search for peace if states, Empires and corporations have neither found an answer nor even asked the question?

This would explain the "mysterious" appearance of NGOs in the political sphere.

Economic Sources of Local Wars

This descent can *begin* as a result of various economic configurations and maintain itself through the militarization of the economy.

In ancient systems or in young states, like in Africa, this descent may start as a penury that "serves a predatory function." The active rekindling of clan and tribal solidarity, that normally provides healthy socio-political guarantees against want or excesses of power, can lead to militarization in cases where a centralized state system falls and its weapons are dispersed. Cohesive identities below the state level then become war-like and enter into a system of reciprocal predatory actions and hoarding of basic goods (as in Somalia). The passage from scarcity to famine derives under these conditions from the state of war, which is itself a cause of famine, and sustains war as a means of communal survival. Africa is currently in the throes of this vicious cycle that transforms a culture of solidarity into one of self-destruction.

In more complex systems that have produced formal states, the initial predatory actions that trigger the entropic catastrophe are more sophisticated, more financial in nature; the *monetary* crises they provoke are more socio-political than communal. Hyperinflation under the Weimar republic led to the rise of Nazism. In our times, the "Mafia" mindset among certain heads of state has lead to the ruin of their banks (in Yugoslavia, the seizure of currency accounts by the Bank of Belgrade; in Albania, the bankruptcy of Mafia pyramid schemes). In Mexico, the collapse of the peso during a 15% devaluation that was prematurely revealed by a leak from inside sources pro- voked the collapse of Mexican bonds, with the risk of a chain reaction of bankruptcy in Latin America and the United States. The U.S. President put a halt to the catastrophe by opening a credit line of $60 billion. Argentina was practically destroyed and rebuilt by the Falkland Island War, Menemism and hyper- inflation. It may be the only country where the post-Cold War catastrophe led to a "democratic transition," a real dismantling of fascist militarism, though it did so by completely sacrificing the populist left to offensive neoliberalism.

Europe, though most concerned by the matter, was unable to control the consequences of the Yugoslavian and Albanian crashes. It is attempting to do so in Russia with heavy spending, though rather late, since the Mafia pump has been put in place and is sustaining the hemorrhaging. The hope that Putin repre- sents a valve strong enough to allow Russian recapitalization and socio-economic stabilization has taken priority over any hope of immediate profitability, at least for the country's

European neighbors. In this huge mess, the massacres in Chechnya went through profits and losses.

Once upon a time (even in Germany and Japan, with Michelin, etc.), patriarchal and paternalistic corporations were seen as the means of handling class compromises on the corporate level and thereby directly regulating internal peace. But the current global free-market positions are destroying any competence patriarchal companies might have as an instrument of suspending conflict between violent local classes through economic agreements. At present, the disappearance of popular internationalism can be opposed to the establishment of multinational corporations as *political* sovereignties.

Yet human beings are political animals *because they want to live in peace*. Transforming companies into transnational tribes at the elite level is possible, and is a Mafia or sectarian tendency, or even a "noble and cosmopolitan" one, but it contradicts the hiring and lock-out freedom needed to maintain the flexibility of a market economy and this flexibility is also contrary to projects for social peace, since Mafia tribes thrive on war.

The lack of organization in class violence poses obvious problems because it potentially destroys many places where sovereignty can be constructed and therefore social peace, and therefore capital accumulation, to say nothing of democratic peace.

6. Against a Permanent Global War

Is war necessary to recreate a legitimate space for equitable distribution that reestablishes non-predatory identities? Is the threat of war sufficient? The American armed forces and NATO, now the leaders of the global system of repression, have been asking more political questions, either by foundering in a fear of generalized civil war or by questioning the sacrosanct limit between politics and military strategy in order to return to an "anti-globalist" America. Even by taking into account the methodological need for soldiers in charge of reflecting on "future war" to display a certain amount of imagination, the development of a cynical and deadly vision of the future of the world dominated by computerized, interventionist modern armies is disturbing.

For example, in the Summer 1997 issue of the US Army magazine *Parameters*[37] there is an article by a certain Colonel Peters titled "Constant Conflict" that describes the future as follows: there will be no more major wars, but a continuous series of conflicts. These conflicts will mainly oppose "failed" peoples who turn their aggressiveness against each other; in fact American superiority, especially in information technology, and consequently in every domain is now indisputable. This excellence can be considered in neo-Darwinian terms as the superiority of one species that eliminates the other species. American superiority can be found in industry, technology, arms, military capability, but also in our civilization. Our American culture, he went on, is the best and brightest. You can tell since it kills off all others. This absolute superiority that will provide us with overwhelming victories over all our adversaries and rivals will also attract animosity. Peoples frustrated by this domination will probably grow to hate us. We will have to defend ourselves. And this, he concuded, means a good amount of killing.

Paradoxically, there are simultaneous pangs of conscience within the professional military, who tend on the contrary to describe American civilization as being on the verge of collapse. An article in the December 1994 *Marine Corps Gazette* warned, in accordance with other conservative thinking, that "the program (of far-left cultural actors) has slowly become codified as a new ideology, known as 'multiculturalism' or 'politically correct' culture, which is essentially a transfer of Marxism from the society to culture" but it notably concludes: "the next real war we will wage will no doubt take place on American soil."[38] Similar remarks were penned by another retired colonel a few months later. Colonel Michael Wyly wrote that "we must be prepared to recognize that our real enemy could just as well appear within our borders as outside them."[39]

This fear of civil war is one of the themes developed by two other authors, acolytes of absolute American superiority through technology, the Töfflers.[40] They esteem that the clash between agricultural and industrial civilizations has already taken place in the United States during the Civil War. But the clash between industrial civilization and computer civilization is yet to come and could take the form of a civil war inside the United States and elsewhere in the world.

It is important to understand that a certain wing of American ideology and, perhaps soon Euro-American, is leading towards a swirling black hole, a destructive fatality, an ideology of absolute superiority of the West over the rest of the world. For Europeans who have already paid dearly for the right to criticize military excesses as they develop, it is important to take the necessary precautions to furnish, create and impose if need be, another direction for human civilization around the globe. But how?

Citizen Protests

Ever since the final phase of the Cold War, citizen movements have proven that they can influence the course of the world most effectively by supporting clear ethical positions. This is how I interpret the German *Friedensbewegung* that put an end to the race for a new generation of medium-range nuclear weapons (Pershing II and SS20); their deployment in Central Europe would have surely rejuvenated the idea of a nuclear arms race and of limited nuclear war. Rather than a new race, public opinion rejected this modernization and, by the same token, the absurd logic that claimed to ensure German security with the threat of the complete destruction of Germany in the first few hours of conflict.

This refusal marked the beginning of the end of the arms race and the real end of the Cold War, since German pacifism convinced the Soviet elite, and especially the military, that they could try to slow down the arms race and completely reform the Russian system of production without the risk of a surprise American attack.

A provisional form of "negentropic" protest adopted recently in the French Republic is the claim of a "citizen" identity that reaches beyond divisions and party lines: citizens in fact represent the Sovereign, the source of the future state. Because of the hellish descent triggered by the call for a "tribal" France by the National Front, they were, as a result, placed under political surveillance. The majority of the French people see themselves as possessing a detribalized citizenship, but are still waiting for a new social compact, a new socio-economic *foedus*, a new political system.

This compact cannot be sealed on the level of nation-states precisely because nation-state institutions are in the process of undoing popular national sovereignty under the pressure of globalization. The new *foedus* cannot come from corporations either, since their only social compact is profit seeking, or from multinational corporations, let alone from the distant power of the American Empire.

As a result, secular and citizens of the French Republic demand European federalism for specific reasons that are distinct from their German, Italian and English counterparts. However, if the fusion of the European political space does occur, it will not originate from a decision from on high, but in the political debates that are imposed by a number of different schools, within the general form of the left-right opposition and of social regulation of the economy. A long populist tradition will renew these political forms in Europe. These debates will then influence part of the global economy in power and create a critical mass of citizens large enough to cross the Atlantic and penetrate other continents by competing with American ideologies of consumerism and profit as well as with the heavy persistence of despotism, "enlightened" at best, that dominates most of Eurasia.

III

CONCLUSIONS

Once the fall of the USSR was revealed by Soviet abstention from the Gulf War, humanity for the first time experienced a true globality, in other words, the reciprocal enactment of a world economy and what could be called "world-violence": *the coexistence of a globalized world economy and a strategic system based on the presence of a single dominant military Empire.* This globality, however, is not real. It is only virtual, or imaginary.

It is true that the past decade has seen the dawn of a new era. For the Americans, it is truly new: they believe we have *really* entered the era of the global economy. The only state *truly* opposed to the global expansion of capitalism was the Soviet Empire. The world is therefore truly unified by the criteria of market economies. The remnants of "state" or "controlled" economies are leftovers that the United States has explicitly acted to eliminate through arguments or force. Still, to obtain the ideal globality, nation-states must be destroyed as a legitimate level of economic regulation, despite the fact that nation-states were once useful tools in the preceding phase of expanding the global economy by allowing national bourgeoisies and protected national markets to intertwine. Relationships of power and the political competition that formed within them *corresponded* more or less to competitive market relationships, since there were national bourgeoisies and corporations, be they public or private, and protected national markets.

The elimination of nations, except the American nation, of course, will lead to misery and disorder if no alternative political program appears. Yet the United States precisely offers no program. Liberalism remains silent concerning the shape of the state, except in favor of electoral democracy and what is know as "good governance"; however, no one has seen a democracy that was not part of a nation-state, and "good governance" is the *result* of political and social activity, not their cause. It is not a definition of state power *under liberalism*. Some would like to see the non-intervention of the state in economic affairs to be the definition of "good governance," but this illusion does not even work for banks of issue. Representative assemblies are part of the state and private, state elites constantly intervene in economic policy.

Only private, multinational corporations are outside the state, but they are also outside democracy. This internal contradiction in American ideology is irremediable. It is too obvious to pass for artistic vagueness or empirical prudence; it represents a veritable intellectual and moral dead-end that everyone can see. Some people pretend to ignore the problem for imperial discourse out of politeness or sycophancy. In fact, as we will see in the sequences of decisions made in the urgency of cruel little wars, the Empire is timid. Is it not in the process of organizing leadership through chaos?

"Leadership" through Chaos?

"World leadership through chaos," a doctrine that a rational European school would have difficulty imagining, necessarily leads to weakening states—even the United States—through the emerging *sovereignty* of corporations and markets.

In fact, for structural or variable economic reasons, the final agreement, the Compact, Peace is not always the goal pursued by the United States. This remark has already been made, even by the Israelis and Palestinians during the direct, bilateral negotiations in Oslo; the absence of the United States, and thus of the pressures of the American pro-Israel lobby, contributed to accelerating the agreement. Negotiations were held, under UN authority, *between the warlords of Somalia* themselves *to rebuild the state*, presided by the Algerian ambassador Sahnoun, the UN mediator who served as a mere facilitator representing no relationship of force. The negotiations, however, were brought to a standstill by Washington because the United States did not want *autonomous* peace in Africa, a peace that did not follow American rules. The fate of the Palestinian peace process is the most telling in terms of the mechanisms of failure induced by the excessive power of American "mediation."

The United States and Europe

We now come to the main preoccupation of our "anthropological" description of wars. The decade following the end of the Gulf War revealed the existence of seldom explicit conflict in Euro-American criteria for certain local struggles. No progress can be made on the path to peace unless this debate is brought to light. If Europe wishes to establish peace agreements at a different pace, with different contents in zones where it has well-defined security interests and its diplomatic expertise has not diminished, it will have to equip itself with the means to influence these now vicious processes and to rekindle lasting peace. It will only be able to do so by clearly stating its differences with the United States when they exist.

This does not mean perpetually relying on powerless judicial formalism, even in the form of UN resolutions, but rather remaining faithful to the desire to create political order by means of agreements between parties, without neglecting the fact that the relationship between military forces is part of the relationship of political forces while accepting that the relationship between military forces cannot *constitute* political agreement. The goal and usefulness of outside participants is precisely to modify impossible local agreements by introducing a relationship to external forces that serves to redistribute strength equally in conflicts that are too asymmetrical to find an equitable agreement.

Europe should now make itself heard more clearly: there will be no peace without states in its zones of immediate interest, its neighborhood, the Balkans, the Mediterranean. This definition will serve as a principal strategic foundation, even if it is necessary to contribute to the creation of new states in the Balkans, then re-federate them. Europe should make clear that America is mistaken in its search for military space without sovereignty, peace without pacts and economic space without politics. If the United States does not change its ways in the South, in Bosnia, in Kosovo, in Israel, in Colombia, it will only create new and rampant "Russian Mafias."

NOTES

1. Strategic theory has been defined—and illustrated—by General Lucien Poirier in his *Essais de stratégie théorique*. Paris: Fondation pour les études de Defense nationale, coll. Les Sept épées, 1982, reprinted in *Stratégie théorique I, II*. Paris: Economica, 1987, 1994.

2. Machiavelli, *First Ten Books of Livy*, Book 2.

3. Hannah Arendt, "Thinking and Moral Considerations: a Lecture," *Social Research*, vol. 38, n. 3, Autumn 1971, p. 417-446.

4. This "forever" ended, however, when Diocletian separated the Eastern and Western empires and decided to reign from Nicea in Asia Minor, calling himself Jupiterian while the Western Empire was left to a secondary emperor named "Herculian," the first of whom was Diocletian's colleague Maximien, also originally from Illyria, the region located at the boundary at the Roman and Greek worlds. Later, the Western Empire fell to barbarian invasions and the Eastern, "Byzantine" Empire survived with its totally Hellenic culture.

5. See John Mueller, "The Banality of Ethnic War," *International Security*, vol 25, n. 1, Summer 2000, p. 42.

6. Cf. Manfred K. Rotermund, *The Fog of Peace: Finding the End-State of Hostilities*. IIS Carlisle Barracks, November 2000.

7. Max Weber, *The Agrarian Sociology of Ancient Civilizations*. New York: Verso, 1988.

8. The World (*Mundus* in Latin; *Kosmos* in Greek means the same thing) signifies clean, elegant, and even cosmetically enhanced as well as Universe. It is a presentable universe, like a cosmetic success.

9. Radio classique (the radio station of French corporate leaders), news bulletin on January 3, 1998.

10. Tacitus, *The Germania*, 33.

11. Two main versions exist in early modern English: "And forgive us our trespasses as we forgive them that trespass against us," *Book of Common Prayer* (1559); "And forgive us our debts, as we also forgive our debters(*sic*)." *The Geneva Bible* (1602, 1607 printing) and *The King James Bible* (1611). [Tn]

12. During the War in Vendée (1793-1796), the republican general Turreau organized his infernal columns to cut a swath of destruction, razing farms, villages in a campaign of terror against royalist supporters. The campaign backfired and general Hoche was sent to quell the revived revolt. [Tn]

13. *Leviathan*, XLVI.

14. With *Behemoth*.

15. In order to analyze power through its most basic tactics and techniques of domination, Foucault recommends abandoning Hobbes: "All in all, we must rid ourselves of the *Leviathan* model, of this model of an artificial man at the same time both manufactured and unified automaton, who encompasses all real individuals and whose citizens would form the body, but whose soul would be sovereignty." Michel Foucault, "*Il Faut défendre la société*"(Society Must be Defended), lecture at the Collège de France, 1976, Hautes Etudes, Gallimard / Seuil, February 1997, p.26.

16. Ibid, p. 28.

17. Fouché, *Memoirs of Joseph Fouché, Duke of Otrante*. Paris: Lerouge libraire, 1824 (2nd edition), p.114-5.

18. *Leviathan*, XXI. Diderot, in the *Encyclopédie*, freely and elegantly translated Hobbes here. He may be reproached for replacing the word *citizen* with *subject* which gives the Sovereign the sense of monarch, whereas Hobbes was careful, in *Leviathan* XVII, not to mention this, calling him a "mortal god," since the Sovereign could theoretically be a single person, a group or an assembly. Hobbes had written in Latin: *Obligatio civium erga eum qui summam habet potestatem tandem nec diutius permanere intelligitur quam manet potentia cives protegendi*, which could be translated word for word as: The citizen's obligation towards he who possesses supreme power isn't expected to outlive his power to protect.

19. *Leviathan*, XXIX: "On Those Things that Weaken or Tend to the *Dissolution* of a Commonwealth"

20. From La Marseillaise:
> Tremble enemies of France:
> Kings drunk with blood and pride,
> The sovereign people is advancing,
> Tyrants prepare your coffins!

21. Marsilius of Padua, *Defensor Pacis*, Discours I, ch. 17 ["On the numerical unity of the supreme government of the state…"] *Medieval Academy Reprints for Teaching*, 1980, p. 80ff.

22. Ibid., I, 19, p. 12.

23. Ibid., I, 19, p. 13.

24. *Leviathan*, XLII.

25. Ibid., XLVII.

26. Ibid., XXXVIII.

27. Cf. John Keegan who develops the question of primitive war at great length in his *A History of Warfare*. New York: Alfred A. Knopf, 1993.
  He even tries to show through the history of the martial decay of Easter Island that Clausewitz is responsible for all militarist self-destruction from the inhabitants of Easter Island to those of Europe because he remarked that

"war is an extension of politics." It is well-known that British scholars of warfare have not forgiven Clausewitz this statement, and Keegan's analysis is close to that of Liddel Hart. Saying that war leads to limitless violence while being at the same time ruled by political reasons, can situate either self-destruction or self-limitation at every level of protection. Clausewitz elaborated the theoretical field of all war but did not publish any recipes for success like Jomini. He takes part in the rare discipline known as theoretical strategy, whereas Keegan uses the fields of the anthropology of regimes and war history for a sociology of combat that is both interesting and worthwhile, but that, as usual, leads to a moral and philosophical reproach of the Prussians for having succeeded in scaring the mighty Great Britain.

28. Jocelyne Barreau, "Les Nouvelles stratégies d'entreprises" [New Corporate Strategies], *Pétition*, no. 2, p. 15.

29. Revised form of a conference presented at the *Dokumenta* exhibit, 1997.

30. Lucien Poirier, *L'Atelier stratégique, entretiens avec Gérard Chaliand* [The Strategic Workshop, Interviews with Gérard Chaliand]. Paris: Hachette (Pluriel), 1997.

31. The Greek word *anachoresis* means "flight into the desert" and was applied to the traditional plebeian-peasant slave revolts in Egypt when they were over-exploited; the flight of the Jews into Sinai is an example. The movement of Christian monks that gave a second meaning to the term was merely a Christian appropriation of this refusal of a world organized for exploitation, and monks in Egypt did form in fact veritable and rather numerous nonconformist societies that were capable of leading violent actions against cities.

32. Both the sphere of production and the exchanges organized within and beyond the strictly military limits of the imperial structure.

33. Immanuel Kant, "Third Definitive Article for Perpetual Peace; Cosmopolitan right shall be limited to conditions of universal hospitality," *Perpetual Peace and other Essays*, trad. Ted Humphrey. Indianapolis: Hackett Publishing Company, 1983, p. 118.

34. cf. A. Philonenko, "Le Problème de la guerre et le machiavélisme chez Fichte" [The Question of War and Machiavellism in Fichte], in *Essais sur la philosophie de la guerre*. Vrin: Paris, 1976. p. 46.

35. In his remarkable introduction to the reprinting of the principles of Human Geography taken from the manuscripts of Vidal de la Blache by de Martonne, Christophe Cordonnier notes how Vidal, contrary to the *Anthropogeography* of Ratzel, did not consider land to be the fixed point to which every explanation should refer, but rather as a "composite medium with the power to group heterogeneous beings and keep them together in cohabitation and reciprocal correlation." Thus "each country represents a domain where disparate beings are artificially united and adapt themselves to life together."

36. Cf. Fukuyama, Francis, *The End of History and the Last Man*. New York: Maxwell Macmillan International, 1992.

37. Ralph Peters, "Constant Conflict," *Parameters*, Summer 1997, pp. 4-14; see also Eliot A. Cohen, "Civil-Military Relations," *Orbis*, vol. 41, n. 2, Spring 1997, pp. 177-186.

38. William S. Lind, *Marine Corps Gazette*, December 1994.

39. Also in the *Marine Corps Gazette*, quoted by Thomas E. Ricks, "The Widening Gap between Military and Society." *The Atlantic Monthly*, July 1997, pp. 66-78.

40. Cf. e.g. Töffler, Alvin and Heidi Töffler, *Creating a New Civilization: the Politics of the Third Wave*. Atlanta: Turner Pub., 1995; or *War and Anti-war: Survival at the Dawn of the Twenty-first Century*. Boston: Little, Brown, 1993.

Printed in the United States
by Baker & Taylor Publisher Services